The Malthus Fraud

The
Malthus
Fraud

Robert Dees

Commons
Press

2023

This book is an excerpt from *The Power of Peasants: Economics and Politics of Farming in Medieval Germany*, by Robert Dees. Houston: Commons Press, 2023.

Printed in Slovakia
First printing 2024
Book and cover design: Tom Tomasko

Front cover: **Two children**. Used with permission of Look and Learn – Historical Picture Archive.
Back cover: Eugène Delacroix. **Liberty Leading the People.** wikipedia.org/wiki/Liberty_Leading_the_People. Public domain.
Gilbert Gaul. **Molly Pitcher at the Battle of Monmouth.** The Union Metallic Cartridge Co. Library of Congress. www.loc.gov/item/2005694435. Public domain.

Commons Press
Website: www.CommonsPress.com
Email: info@CommonsPress.com

CONTENTS

INTRODUCTION

"MOST DISCUSSIONS OF HISTORICAL demography start, continue, and finish with Thomas Malthus."[1] This assessment of the current state of historical analysis, made by a historian who appears to think that this is as it should be, is accurate except that it should not be limited to historical demography. It is true also of much social and political discussion of both past and present. Thomas Malthus's *Essay on the Principle of Population*, by name or simply by approach, is the all-but-ubiquitous explanation for social crises for the precapitalist era and very often is applied to the modern world as well.

Overpopulation is the standard reason given by a broad array of modern historians for the fall in the standard of living of the working population specifically and the crises of the 1300s and 1500s generally.[2] The rise and fall of the Roman Empire and the crisis of 1348, accompanied by the bubonic plague and Hundred Years War, have been attributed to "Malthusian mechanisms."[3] More than one prominent historian has gone so far as to assert that the periodic mass exterminations of over a third of humanity by the plague are to be *thanked* for supposedly having saved the present from the "suffocating pressure of population." "Medieval and Renaissance Europe did not go the way of Asia," one historian claimed, thanks only to the plague.[4] According to a pious economics professor, Gregory Clark, the mass starvation, bubonic plague, and ensuing annihilation were "gifts from God." "War, violence, disorder, harvest failures, collapsed public infrastructures, bad sanitation—were the friends of mankind before 1800. They reduced population pressures and increased material living standards," where-as "peace, stability, order, public health, transfers to the poor—were the enemies of prosperity. They generated the population growth that impoverished societies." The Holo-caust also "reduced population pressures" among Jews, un-der comparably horrific circumstances, and was followed by "increased material living standards," indeed a Jewish cultural Golden Age. Was the Holocaust also a "gift from God," Professor Clark? Not surprisingly, he's the same pro-fessor who claimed that England's success was the result of the genetic superiority of the English upper classes and "its long, peaceful history stretching back to at least 1200 and probably long before."[*5]

Another professor claimed to have "exonerated the [Roman] republic's political leaders from culpability" in the destruction of Rome's small farmers.[6] According to him, the farmers destroyed themselves through overpopulation! In reality, Rome's free farmers were destroyed by centuries of being drafted into the armies and sent to die on the front lines, crushing taxation and indebtedness, and theft of their land by the large landowners.[**]

---

* On the reality of England's long, violent history, see Dees, *Power of Peasants*, "England," in chap. 12.

** For a fuller discussion, see Dees, *Power of Peasants*, chap. 1, "Rome."

Putting aside his ludicrous claims that Rome suffered from overpopulation and that its farmers did themselves in, he did put his finger on the key issue: finding a scapegoat to exonerate the political leaders from guilt for the misery they cause is the whole point of the Malthus fraud.

The worsening conditions from the late 1500s to the early 1600s have been attributed to a "Malthusian situation": "constantly growing population numbers resulted in malnutrition," claimed one authority.[7] Another wrote that "around 1560 the land available for new settlers was in some places exhausted. The wave of population had led to a tremendous growth of the sub-peasant layers, to the appearance of pauperism . . . to ecological overuse."[8] Malthus "remains valid today, particularly for the poor countries of the world," claimed another. According to this line of thinking, overpopulation is a threat not just to poor countries; "the degradation of the environment that is associated with the unprecedented increase in population since World War II threatens, not only to impede progress in the Third World, but to impede, if not reverse, the progress of the OECD world,"[9] referring to the advanced capitalist countries.

There aren't many Jews in the semicolonial world, so supporters of capitalism have to find another scapegoat. Overpopulation is the standard pretext used in the capitalist media—of those countries whose banks drain the wealth of semicolonial countries—to explain the latter's poverty.[10] A variant of this doctrine is used to rationalize the attack on pensions for retirees, alleging that there are too many old people relative to the number still working and paying taxes. "Demographic Time Bomb Threatens Pensions in Europe," warned the *New York Times*, in but one example among hundreds of hysterical headlines in this vein that have appeared in recent years.[11] Some historians recognize that Malthus's "prophecies were proved false," but nevertheless are unable or unwilling to take into account the role of property and class relations. In the end, these writers often paint themselves back into the corner of a basically Malthusian argument to explain food and other social crises.[12]

Thomas Robert Malthus was born in 1766 to English landholding gentry, the lowest level of those who owned enough land that they did not have to work for a living; they rented their land out to working farmers and lived off the rents. His family was just beneath the lowest level of the titled aristocrats and yearned to be socially accepted by them. They tried to prove their worth by conducting themselves toward their titled superiors with fawning servility* and treating their subordinates—those who actually worked for a living—with all the more contempt. But Malthus was the youngest son, so he was not going to inherit the family estate. Malthus was no Cromwell, however. He was not about to stoop to working for a living so, like many before him, he sought a cushy position in the Church. At age twenty-three, he took orders in the Church of England and became assistant pastor in Wotten, Surrey. However, he spent little time caring for souls and much time on his ideological career, which proved to be more lucrative.

"Poverty and misery aris[e] from a too rapid increase of population," and "population has this constant tendency to increase beyond the means of subsistence," alleged Malthus. "The human species," he claimed, increases geometrically, the food supply arithmetically, so population "would increase as the numbers 1, 2, 4, 8, 16, 32, 64, 128, 256, and subsistence as 1, 2, 3, 4, 5, 6, 7, 8, 9. In two centuries the population would be to the means of subsistence as 256 to 9." The fact that this is physically impossible—the population cannot surpass the food supply 256 to 9—has had no effect on the popularity of

---

* Well depicted in the character William Collins in Jane Austin's *Pride and Prejudice*.

Malthus's fraud among modern historians.

Malthus also insisted that his "principle" of population revealed the will of God and was a law of nature, like gravity, impervious to change by government action, revolution, medicine, or technological advances. Those who actually read Malthus's text discover that his argument was essentially religious, a fact left out by virtually all his modern acolytes: violation of his *principle* of population was a violation of *God*'s will. He then grafted on his mathematical formula to give his religious dogma a pseudoscientific veneer.

The cause of the crises in Europe after 1348 and in Germany culminating in the Thirty Years War was the greed of the lords and the stagnant social and property relations they had successfully defended in repeated wars against challenge from below. The main thesis counterposed to this explanation in history texts today is the Malthus doctrine of overpopulation: the lords were completely innocent; the common people did it to themselves by reproducing like rabbits. The data available for Germany disprove this on every point.

1. *The population never outstripped the food supply.* In the second third of the 1400s, the population was rising, but food production rose even faster, as shown by the falling prices. In average years during the 1500s, German farmers produced triple what was needed to feed themselves. Even during the worst famine of the century, 1570–71, German farmers produced at least double what was needed.*

2. *Rising population was not the cause of the crisis of the late 1500s because the population in Germany was falling during this period.* Population necessarily followed the curve of agricultural production, meaning it was probably stagnant through the first half of the

---

* See Dees, *Power of Peasants*, chap. 10.

century and was declining through most of the second half of the 1500s and early 1600s; birth and death records prove this. According to the Malthus doctrine, this falling population should have resulted in economic upturn; in reality, catastrophe ensued.

Thus, both halves of Malthus's formula, on population and food supply, were false. But in its time and since, Malthus's *Essay on Population* has enjoyed extraordinary success. Marx pointed out that it is "one of the most remarkable literary examples of the success of plagiarism at the cost of the original work." [13] So why has such a patently absurd, easily refutable, plagiarized thesis become the standard, all but unique analytical tool in demographic historiography, with wide application in social policy today as well? Answering this question requires a thorough examination of Malthus's argument and the political context in which it was formulated.

POLITICAL CONTEXT

THE FIRST EDITION OF MALTHUS'S treatise was published in 1798—nine years after the French Revolution exploded onto the stage of world history, overthrowing the French monarchy, announcing the doom of feudal rule across Europe, and frightening the bourgeois aristocrats of Britain. Shortly before that, Britain had been defeated by a bunch of colonial rabble in a long and bitter war, making the threat of uprising at home only too real. This was, one historian wrote,

> a time of aroused political passions, the hottest fanaticism, the sharpest partisanship. . . . There was no calm research and consideration—it was a matter of decisive engagement for or against the new. All of Europe was split into two great camps, which furiously battled each other. [14]

"Everything," recalled Lord Cockburn, "not this thing or that thing, but literally everything, was soaked in this one event."[15]

Britain was well into the Industrial Revolution. The British navy ruled the waves abroad, and at home industrial production was growing rapidly. The value of cotton textile exports increased 3.6 times over in a single decade, 1790–1800; pig iron production leapt by more than 3.5 times from 1788 to 1806. Coal production jumped nearly 90 percent from 1785 to 1815, and principal imports soared more than three times over from 1784 to 1831.[16] The national income had more than tripled in the previous fifty years alone.[17] The ruling class enjoyed wealth and power of which their predecessors in 1500 could not even have dreamed.

But this fabulous new wealth did not benefit all. For the farmers and workers who produced it, conditions had gotten much worse; wages were falling. By 1800, the ruling class had successfully driven the real wages of working people down to half what they were in the late 1400s.[18] "Wretched, defrauded, oppressed, crushed human nature lying in bleeding fragments all over the face of society," wrote a foreign observer. "Every day that I live I thank Heaven that I am not a poor man with a family in England."[19] (These lines were written in 1845, by which time real wages had nearly doubled over what they were in 1800.) In his book, Malthus used "the poor," "the lower classes," and "the labouring classes" interchangeably. This accurately described the condition of working people then prevailing in England, which his essay argued should be preserved and worsened.

Not surprisingly, the misery into which the rulers had reduced the toilers who produced their wealth, together with the examples set by the American and French Revolutions, propelled a wave of unrest in England. Lady Shelley wrote in her diary, "The awakening of the labouring classes, after the first shock of the French Revolution, made the upper classes tremble. They began to fear that those who had hitherto been treated as helots might one day, as in France, get the upper hand."*[20] There were demonstrations in England celebrating the victories of the French armies. William Wilberforce, a member of parliament, received a report in 1792 that

> during the late disturbances amongst the keelmen . . . General Lambton was thus addressed: "Have you read this little work of Tom Paine's [*The Rights of Man*]?" "No." "Then read it—we like it much. You have a great estate, General; we shall soon divide it amongst us."

During the 1795 famine, the prominent politician Edmund Burke preached: "Patience, labour, sobriety, frugality and religion, should be recommended" to the working class.[21] Teach them to starve quietly. However, "miners, potters and cutlers reading *Rights of Man*" and "working men in villages and towns over the whole country [were] claiming *general* rights for themselves. It was this—and not the French Terror—which threw the propertied classes into panic," one historian pointed out."**[22]

As Malthus put it,

> an idea has lately prevailed among some of the lower classes of society, that the land is the people's farm, the rent of which ought to be equally divided among them; and that they have been deprived of the benefits which belong to them from this their natural inheritance, by the injustice

---

* In ancient Sparta, most farmers were helots, an especially harsh form of slavery.

** Thomas Paine participated in the American Revolution of 1776. His pamphlet *Common Sense* advocated independence from Britain. His later pamphlet *The Rights of Man* denounced hereditary aristocracy and defended the French Revolution of 1789 from British intellectual critics.

and oppression of their stewards, the landlords.[23]

Even more frightening to him was the

popular tumult, the members of which (at least the greater number of them) were persuaded that the destruction of the Parliament, the Lord Mayor, and the monopolizers, would make bread cheap, and that a revolution would enable them all to support their families.[24]

"Waves of desperation broke time and again over the country" in what became "pervasive social and political unrest." The discontent rose to near revolutionary proportions; "no period of British history has been as tense, as politically and socially disturbed, as the 1830s and early 1840s." This wave of protest culminated in the formation of early trade unions, the organization of the mass Chartist movement in 1838,[25] and in 1848 renewed outbreak of revolution across the continent and the formation of the modern communist workers movement.

The government responded to the broad enthusiasm among working people for the French Revolution with repression. Leaders of reform societies were arrested for treason, and "printers, publishers, writers and booksellers were prosecuted for their production and circulation of radical works—particularly of Paine's *Rights of Man*."[26] Paine was convicted in England, in his absence, of seditious libel against the monarchy and sentenced to hang, but alas could not be captured.

The defeat of the British government at the hands of American revolutionaries and of the French monarchy by the laboring classes inspired confidence among British working people and fear among the elites. This posed the need for an ideological counteroffensive. Enter Malthus. The *Essay on Population* was Malthus's contribution to this battle of ideas. It was and continues to be nothing but a defense of the status quo and class-based privilege, an attempt to divert people's attention from the real cause of their misery, and an attack on the aspirations for human equality aroused by revolutions.

This is not a tendentious reading of Malthus's text. Malthus clearly stated his objective: "the principal argument of this essay, only goes to prove the necessity of a class of proprietors, and a class of labourers." [27] The *principal* argument.

The full title of the first edition of his book is *An Essay on the Principle of Population, as it Affects the Future Improvement of Society, with Remarks on the Speculations of Mr. Godwin, M. Condorcet, and Other Writers*. The opening lines of the preface read: "The following Essay owes its origin to a conversation with a friend, on the subject of Mr. Godwin's Essay, on avarice and profusion in his Enquirer." [28] In this first edition, six of the nineteen chapters were devoted to responding to William Godwin.

Godwin was the author of *An Enquiry Concerning Political Justice*, published in 1793, and *The Enquirer* in 1797. His defense of the French Revolution and attacks on class privilege briefly catapulted Godwin into extraordinary prominence in the white-hot polemics then raging in England. [29] Not coincidentally, Godwin was also the husband of Mary Wollstonecraft, the most prominent advocate of women's rights of her time and author of *A Vindication of the Rights of Man*, in response to Edmund Burke's attack on the French Revolution, and *A Vindication of the Rights of Woman*, in which she pointed out that the "inferiority" of women results from their lack of education, not nature. Godwin and Wollstonecraft had met at a gathering that included the firebrand Thomas Paine. Her previous lover—in Paris, where she had gone to witness the revolution firsthand—had been a captain in the American revolutionary army. [30]

Malthus also named the Marquis de Condorcet, a pamphleteer for the French Revolution who believed in the infinite perfectibility of humanity and that over time inequality among nations and classes would be erased.[31]

After the government suppressed one round of unrest in England, Malthus wrote that "the actual disposition of the government to tyranny" was motivated by fear on the part of the gentry that "the common people . . . should by any revolutionary movement obtain an ascendant." Part of the problem, he explained, was "the circulation of Paine's Rights of Man," which "has done great mischief among the lower and middling classes of people in this country."[32] It was against polemicists like Godwin and Paine, women like Wollstonecraft, and the welcome that the American and French Revolutions found among working people in Britain that Malthus aimed his attack.

THE IDEOLOGY

POVERTY CAUSED BY LAW OF NATURE
GODWIN ARGUED THAT

> the spirit of oppression, the spirit of servility, and the spirit of fraud, these are the immediate growth of the established administration of property. They are alike hostile to intellectual improvement. The other vices of envy, malice, and revenge, are their inseparable companions. In a state of society where men lived in the midst of plenty, and where all shared alike the bounties of nature, these sentiments would inevitably expire.[33]

Malthus responded,

> the great bent of Mr. Godwin's work on political justice . . . is

to shew, that the greater part of the vices and weaknesses of men, proceed from the injustice of their political and social institutions: and that if these were removed, and the understandings of men more enlightened, there would be little or no temptation in the world to evil. As has been clearly proved, however, (at least as I think) that this is entirely a false conception, and that, independent of any political or social institutions whatever, the greater part of mankind, from the fixed and unalterable laws of nature, must ever be subject to the evil temptations arising from want, besides other passions.[34]

"From the fixed and unalterable laws of nature" comes straight from Aristotle's natural law, which taught that slavery and the oppression of women were immutable laws of nature.[35] Of course, the claim that class domination is "human nature" is at least half true. Marx did point out that it is people's "social existence that determines their consciousness."[36] In antiquity, the master-slave relationship was human nature; under feudalism, the lord-serf relationship was human nature; under capitalism, the capitalist-proletarian relationship is human nature. But if you accept these three truths, then you have accepted the fact that human nature changes depending on the mode of production, because now we already have three "human natures," each of which developed by overthrowing the previous. And once you've accepted that, it follows that it is also human nature for slaves to slit their masters' throats, for serfs to rebel against their lords, and for workers to rise up against the capitalists; it's just human nature.

Marx noted that "the materialist doctrine that people are products of circumstances and upbringing, and that, therefore, changed people are products of other circumstances and changed upbringing, forgets that it is people who change circumstances."[37] As we've seen on this

voyage,* from Spartacus to the overthrow of Roman slavery, the early rebellions against the tithe, the Morgarten
peasants, the Legnano townspeople, the Hussite rebels, the
Drummer of Niklashausen, the Bundschuh conspiracies,
the Peasant War, the American and French Revolutions
and since, the fight against oppression and for equality is
also irrepressible human nature, at least among those who
work for a living.

Malthus, however, insisted that the "laws of nature" were
impervious to change. "No change of government could
essentially better their condition," he insisted, and "a revolution would not alter in their favour the proportion of the
supply of labour to the demand, or the quantity of food to
the number of the consumers." Attempting to change this
state of affairs is futile, for "man cannot live in the midst of
plenty. All cannot share alike the bounties of nature." Indeed, these laws were not just the laws of nature, but "are
the laws of God," thundered Reverend Malthus.[38] This
hoary relic was plagiarized from the pharaohs of Egypt. It
didn't work for them either.

Malthus countered Godwin's argument with his "principle of population."

> The principal and most permanent cause of poverty has lit-
> tle or no relation to forms of government, or the unequal
> division of property; and that, as the rich do not in reality
> possess the power of finding employment and maintenance
> for the poor, the poor cannot, in the nature of things, pos-
> sess the right to demand them, are important truths flow-
> ing from the principle of population.[39]

To repeat: "The principal and most permanent cause
of poverty has . . . no relation to . . . the unequal division of

---

* See Dees, *Power of Peasants.*

property." That otherwise intelligent people can read lines like that and docilely nod their heads in reverence is a monument to the mental blindness that flows from professorial venality.

According to Malthus, workers' demands for work, unemployment compensation, and other poor relief violate the laws of nature and are contrary to God's will. Malthus argued that

> from the inevitable laws of our nature, some human beings *must* suffer from want. These are the unhappy persons who, in the great lottery of life, have drawn a blank. . . . [For according to] the principle of population, more will always be in want than can adequately be supplied.[40]

Misery forever, from the fixed and unalterable laws of nature, was Malthus's position. The penalty for violation of this law of nature was harsh. Malthus explained that working people

> should be taught to know that the laws of nature, which are the laws of God, had doomed him and his family to starve for disobeying their repeated admonitions; that he had no claim of right on society for the smallest portion of food, beyond that which his labour would fairly purchase.[41]

In his new position as parish pastor, he observed that

> the sons and daughters of peasants will not be found such rosy cherubs in real life, as they are described to be in romances. It cannot fail to be remarked by those who live much in the country, that the sons of labourers are very apt to be stunted in their growth, and are a long while arriving at maturity. Boys that you would guess to be fourteen or fifteen, are, upon enquiry, frequently found to be eighteen or nineteen.[42]

As far as Malthus was concerned, these children were still

getting too much; they should be done away with completely: "The laws of God, had doomed him and his family to starve." Left out of Malthus's analysis is the fact that he never did a day's labor in his life. After his cushy position as personal pastor in the private chapel of a wealthy family, he went on to become a professional propagandist for the landowning aristocracy, who also did no work. The whole point was to keep it that way.

In addition, Malthus argued that although the government was "impotent in its efforts to make the food of a country keep pace with an unrestricted increase of population, yet its influence is great in giving the best direction to those checks, which in some form or other must necessarily take place."[43] Malthus alleged that "preventive" and "positive" checks were two laws of nature that restrict population growth and that should be promoted by government action.

PREVENTIVE CHECK: SEXUAL REPRESSION

MALTHUS'S PREVENTIVE CHECK consisted of the sexual oppression of the working and rural classes in general and of women in particular. This oppression should be enforced, according to Malthus, by the threat of starvation, condemnation by God, and government action. "Moral restraint, till we are in a condition to support a family, is the strict line of duty."[44]

> There are perhaps few actions that tend so directly to diminish the general happiness as to marry without the means of supporting children. He who commits this act, therefore, clearly offends against the will of God; and having become a burden on society . . . violated his duty to his neighbors and to himself, and thus to have listened to the voice of passion in opposition to his higher obligations.[45]

By "moral restraint," Malthus meant no sex for the

toilers before marriage and no marriage until the worker had found guaranteed lifetime employment that paid
enough to support a family. The fact that working-class
jobs that paid such wages were almost nonexistent in
England at the time and that no worker under capitalism
ever has guaranteed lifetime employment did not impinge
upon his illogic. "The interval between the age of puber-
ty and the period at which each individual might venture
on marriage must . . . be passed in strict chastity; because
the law of chastity cannot be violated without producing
evil." [46] (Is this your experience?)

But convincing working people that practicing normal
sexuality was a violation of God's will and an assault on
the state was not based solely or even primarily on con-
cern that it might produce surplus population. Enjoying
sex, even if it produced no babies, was also illicit, at least
for workers. "I have little doubt that there have been some
irregular connexions with women which have added to the
happiness of both parties, and have injured no one. These
individual actions . . . are still evidently vicious," Malthus
pontificated, because "no person can doubt the general
tendency of an illicit intercourse between the sexes to in-
jure the happiness of society." He hammered repeatedly at
this point. [47]

As society's lords had learned, convincing young people to give up sex was no easy task; convincing them to
do so merely to solidify the rulers' property relations was
impossible. The lash of Church morality had to be applied.
Malthus's "morality" served as an internal enforcement
mechanism, self-enslaving every individual who could be
deceived into believing that sex was inherently immoral and
sinful. This goes back to Plato's slaveholder ideology, advo-
cating making working people feel ashamed of sex, then using this shame as a weapon of control. [48]

POSITIVE CHECKS: STARVATION, DISEASE, WAR

MALTHUS ADVOCATED "SQUALID POVERTY" and star-vation to prevent "a great number of persons in all civilized nations from pursuing the dictate of nature in an early at-tachment to one woman."[49] "If any man chose to marry, without a prospect of being able to support a family," Malthus insisted, he should be left to "the punishment, therefore, of nature . . . the punishment of severe want."[50] "If he cannot support his children, they must starve."[51]

> A man who is born into a world already possessed, if he cannot get subsistence from his parents on whom he has a just demand, and if the society do not want his labour, has no claim of *right* to the smallest portion of food, and, in fact, has no business to be where he is. At nature's mighty feast there is no vacant cover for him. She tells him to be gone, and will quickly execute her own orders . . . the in-fant is, comparatively speaking, of no value to the society, as others will immediately supply its place.[52]

Malthus argued that starvation was the natural consequence of a rising population. He also strongly opposed even ad-vances in medicine that might get in the way of famine and disease working as weapons to keep the toilers in their place.

Smallpox it is believed to have killed more people throughout history than any other infectious disease—in-cluding the bubonic plague—and was still a leading cause of death in England in 1800. In 1796, Edward Jenner developed a vaccine against it using a related cowpox virus that af-fected cattle but produced only mild symptoms in humans. Jenner, however, was trained not as an academic at a uni-versity but by practical apprenticeship to a country surgeon. The next year, when he submitted his paper describing this historic breakthrough, the Royal Society rejected it. Never-theless, Jenner's technique spread rapidly.

Malthus and many other churchmen opposed it and any pursuit of scientific solutions to the problems facing humanity as attempts to subvert God's will.[53] He acknowledged that

> millions and millions of human beings have been destroyed by the small-pox. [It] is certainly one of the channels, and a very broad one, which nature has opened for the last thousand years, to keep down the population to the level of the means of subsistence; but had this been closed, others would have become wider, or new ones would have been formed. . . . If the introduction of the cow-pox should extirpate the small-pox, and yet the number of marriages continue the same, we shall find a very perceptible difference in the increased mortality of some other diseases.[54]

"Nature will not, nor cannot, be defeated in her purposes," Malthus insisted.

> The necessary mortality must come in some form or other; and the extirpation of one disease will only be the signal for the birth of another, perhaps more fatal. We cannot lower the waters of misery by pressing them down in different places which must necessarily make them rise somewhere else.[55]

Disease, like poverty, Malthus pretended, was God's penalty for violating the law of nature. "Diseases have been generally considered as the inevitable inflictions of Providence; but, perhaps, a great part of them may more justly be considered as indications that we have offended against some of the laws of nature."[56] Malthus pursued his argument to its monstrous but logical conclusion.

> To act consistently, therefore, we should facilitate, instead of foolishly and vainly endeavouring to impede the

operations of nature, in producing this mortality; and if we dread the too frequent visitation of the horrid form of famine, we *should sedulously encourage the other forms of destruction* which we compel nature to use. Instead of recommending cleanliness to the poor, we should encourage contrary habits. In our towns we should make the streets narrower, crowd more people into the houses, and court the return of the plague. In the country we should build our villages near stagnant pools, and particularly encourage settlement in all marshy and unwholesome situations. But above all, we should reprobate [strongly condemn] specific remedies for ravaging diseases, and those benevolent, but much mistaken men, who have thought they were doing a service to mankind by projecting schemes for the total extirpation of particular disorders.[57]

If nothing else, Malthus was utterly consistent. His opposition to using science and medicine to improve the human condition snapped precisely into place with the rest of his ideology like the pieces of a close-fitting puzzle. It was the natural continuation of the long history of the ruling elite's fear of a scientific understanding of nature and society that continues to this day.

REFORMERS: OWEN AND YOUNG

IN ADDITION TO OPPOSING advances in medicine to improve the lot of the toilers, Malthus also fought political moves to that end, even reform proposals such as those of Robert Owen and Arthur Young. Owen advocated "a community of labour and of goods."[58] Malthus opposed this for two reasons. First "is the unsuitableness of a state of equality . . . to the production of those stimulants to exertion which can alone overcome the natural indolence of man, and prompt him to the proper cultivation of the earth."[59] Malthus saw inequality in society and the resulting starvation as necessary prods to making the toilers work. He did not mention what prods could be brought to bear to overcome the landlords' indolence. His second reason was based on "the inevitable and necessary poverty and misery in which every system of equality must shortly terminate from the acknowledged tendency of the human race to increase faster than the means of subsistence."

Setting aside for the moment the lie that the human race increases faster than the means of subsistence, Malthus's reasoning ran as follows: A system of equality would without doubt result in more food for the toilers. But "the encouragement and motive to moral restraint [that is, no sex] are at once destroyed in a system of equality and community of goods."[60] So, if working people actually had enough to eat, they would only reproduce faster than the food supply.

Arthur Young, an agronomist and contemporary of Malthus, proposed as a way "to prevent future scarcities so oppressive to the poor as the present . . . to secure to every country labourer . . . half an acre of land for potatoes, and grass enough to feed one or two cows." This, too, Malthus opposed for the same reason—if the toilers have enough to eat, they will reproduce faster, only compounding the problem. Malthus even opposed proposals to establish foundling homes for infants.[61]

KEEP THEM POOR

BUT THE "PRINCIPLE OF POPULATION" was not the only reason (nor even the real reason) Malthus advocated keeping the working class poor.

> If a tract of rich land as large as this island [Britain] were suddenly annexed to it, and sold in small lots, or let out in small farms . . . the amelioration of the state of the common people would be sudden and striking; though the rich would be continually complaining of the high price of

labour, the pride of the lower classes, and the difficulty of getting work done. These, I understand, are not unfrequent complaints among the men of property in America.[62]

The problem was not merely that a living wage would lead to over-reproduction. "It is a general complaint among master manufacturers that high wages ruin all their workmen,"[63] Malthus whined—at a time when wages in England were close to a fifty-year low and per capita food consumption was falling.[64]

Thus, according to Malthus, well-off workers are too proud. Making them work hard requires keeping them desperately poor. What he was too blind to see was that the higher wages, relatively greater freedom, and uppity attitude of the farmers and workers in the US were the main *reasons* for its accelerated development. He also opposed trade unions and labor's drive "to combine, with a view to keep up the price of labour and to prevent persons from working below a certain rate. But such combinations [trade unions] are not only illegal, but irrational and ineffectual."* [65]

Protecting the private property of the rich requires starving the poor out of wanting sex, because "the first grand requisite to the growth of prudential habits is the perfect security of property."[66] In order for the mass of working people to have "prudential habits" (little sex and hard work), the wealthy few must have "perfect security of property" and the workers none. As Malthus pointed out accurately, "When these two fundamental laws of society, the security of property and the institution of marriage, were once established, inequality of conditions must necessarily follow."[67] Indeed, the institution of marriage was created to concentrate property in fewer hands.**

---

* On why trade unions are not only rational but essential, see Marx, "Trades' Unions."

** See Dees, *Power of Peasants*, "Marriage and inheritance," in chap. 4.

Malthus also strongly opposed abortion and birth control, or as he termed it, "improper arts to conceal the consequences of irregular connexions" or that "prevents the birth of children." He was hostile to allowing couples any control over the number of children they had because of "their tendency to remove a necessary stimulus to industry. If it were possible for each married couple to limit by a wish the number of their children, there is certainly reason to fear that the indolence of the human race would very greatly be increased." [68]

Opposition to birth control might seem odd for someone who claimed that misery was caused by overpopulation. But his position is entirely consistent with the underlying ideology of his argument. Without the ability to manage reproduction, working women can never be truly equal in modern society. The vagaries of uncontrolled births deepen the desperation and therefore the dependency of working women on men, and of both on whatever wages can be had in the frantic scramble to feed their hungry children. This distress naturally promotes their industry, prevents their indolence, drives down wages, and raises employers' profits. Deepening the oppression of women and restricting access to birth control helps advance these goals—a simple reality understood well by Pope Innocent VIII, the witch hunter Heinrich Kramer, Thomas Malthus, and all who would rob women of the right to control their own bodies to this day.

EDUCATION TO KEEP THEM DUMB

MALTHUS ADVOCATED A SYSTEM of general education. "It is surely a great national disgrace, that the education of the lower classes of people in England should be left merely to a few Sunday schools." [69] This too was consistent with his ideology. In the world in which Malthus lived, the toilers of America and France had just risen up in revolutionary struggle, overthrown and expropriated some of their oppressors, and begun improving their condition in life. Knowledge of this experience and an acute sense of injustice were wide-spread among working people in England, in part through the writings of people like Godwin, Paine, and Wollstonecraft. The thrust of Malthus's ideology was, through education/indoctrination, to divert this sense of injustice away from the "unjust institutions of society" and onto the poor themselves.

> When the wages of labour are hardly sufficient to maintain two children, a man marries and has five or six. He of course finds himself miserably distressed. He accuses the insufficiency of the price of labour to maintain a family. He accuses his parish. . . . He accuses the avarice of the rich, who suffer him to want what they can so well spare. He accuses the partial and unjust institutions of society, which have awarded him an inadequate share of the produce of the earth. He accuses perhaps the dispensations of Providence. . . . In searching for objects of accusation, he never adverts to the quarter from which all his misfortunes originate. The last person that he would think of accusing is himself, on whom, in fact, the whole of the blame lies.[70]

Malthus's ideology was a direct continuation of the doctrine claiming that the cause of slavery was sin, and of the ruling-class ideology that working people should not blame their oppressors for their miserable condition but only themselves or, when that did not work, God's will, the Jews, the witches, the weather, or anyone but the real culprits.

In 1525 in Germany, the effectiveness of religion as a tool of social control had been seriously weakened by the rising self-confidence of the mobilized toilers, the moral depravity of the clergy, and the increasingly open conflicts by factions of the ruling classes with the Church. Luther had understood and feared this, and for this reason he too advocated public education, not of the critical, scientific type, but as a supplement to the religious indoctrination of young minds.

By 1800 in England, the decline of the effectiveness of religion as a tool of social control was much more advanced, helped along by the example of two living revolutions and the spread of a scientific understanding of the world revived by Galileo and Newton. Like Luther before him, Reverend Malthus was well situated to be acutely aware that, no matter how furiously he wielded the club of God, religion alone no longer sufficed to hold the people down. Another avenue of indoctrination was needed.

Education's role in indoctrination was recently explained by the capitalist ideologue Douglass North. Capitalist economic theory, he wrote,

> can explain how people acting in their own self-interest behave. . . . It cannot, however, explain . . . behavior in which calculated self-interest is not the motivating factor. How do we account for altruistic behavior? . . . Neoclassical theory is equally deficient in explaining stability. Why do people obey the rules of society when they could evade them to their benefit?

Indeed, "a neoclassical [capitalist] world would be a jungle and no society would be viable"[71] if everyone really acted in their own self-interest, as capitalist "neoclassical" ideology advocates. But as North pointed out, relying on government repression alone to ensure each and every act of compliance with the existing order, posting a cop every few feet, would be ruinously expensive.

> Compliance is so costly that the enforcement of any body of rules in the absence of some degree of individual restraint from maximizing behavior would render the political or economic institution non-viable—hence the enormous investment that is made to convince individuals of the legitimacy of these institutions . . . the measurement costs

of constraining behavior are so high that in the absence of ideological convictions to constrain individual maximizing, the viability of economic organization is threatened.[72]

Translating this professorese into plain English: To reduce the cost of cops and clubs to enforce compliance with the status quo, "ideological convictions"—indoctrination—must be imposed to convince the working majority *not* to act in their own self-interest but to serve the interests of the ruling minority, thereby allowing the latter to maximize *their* interests at the expense of the former. This approach is hardly new; it goes back to the pharaohs of Egypt, who taught the peasants that pharaoh was a god and their miserable lot was the will of the gods. The Roman toady Seneca used it to teach his slaves to stoically accept their condition so that he could wallow without worry in wealth.

Even this is not cheap, as Constantine and subsequent rulers learned. North noted that it requires "enormous investment . . . to convince individuals of the legitimacy of these institutions." But in the end, he acknowledged, it is "military technology" that determines "the underlying terms of exchange (property rights structure) between rulers and constituents."[73] Translation: When the people stop falling for the lies, force is needed to keep them down.

As was the case with Luther and North, the "education" that Malthus advocated served not to educate but to brainwash the lower classes with the rulers' ideology. Patriotism was an important part of it. The toilers were supposed to act contrary to their own interests and serve their exploiters because it was God's will and the law of nature; it was their patriotic duty to serve as cannon fodder so that their exploiters could calmly squeeze them that much more tightly at home and those they conquered abroad. Malthus insisted that a big part of the problem was that the ignorant "laboring classes" simply were unaware that they themselves were the problem.

And till this obscurity is entirely removed, and the poor are undeceived with respect to the principal cause of their past poverty, and taught to know that their future happiness or misery must depend chiefly upon themselves, it cannot be said that, with regard to the great question of marriage or celibacy, we leave every man to his own free and fair choice.[74]

Malthus hoped that such indoctrination would help breed subservience by the toilers to their rulers. If his "truths were . . . more generally known," then

the lower classes of people, as a body, would become more peaceable and orderly; would be less inclined to tumultuous proceedings in seasons of scarcity, and would at all times be less influenced by inflammatory and seditious publications, from knowing how little the price of labour, and the means of supporting a family, depend upon a revolution.[75]

Every man in the lower classes of society, who became acquainted with these truths, would be disposed to bear the distresses in which he might be involved with more patience; would feel less discontent and irritation at the government and the higher classes of society on account of his poverty; would be on all occasions less disposed to insubordination and turbulence.[76]

Even if the miserable condition of the toilers didn't change, ideologically pacifying them would give the rulers a freer hand to pursue its own interests without fear of revolution.

The mere knowledge of these truths, even if they did not operate sufficiently to produce any marked change in the prudential habits of the poor, with regard to marriage, would still have a most beneficial effect on their conduct in a political light; and undoubtedly, one of the most valuable of these effects would be the power that would result to the higher and middle classes of society of gradually improving their governments without the apprehension of those revolutionary excesses.[77]

The French novelist Alexandre Dumas summed up the effect of this sort of schooling: "How is it that little children are so intelligent and most men so stupid? It must be education that does it."[78]

ABOLISH THE POOR LAWS

"THE POOR ARE BY NO MEANS inclined to be visionary," Malthus claimed. It is "among the people of property" where "improvements in government must necessarily originate."[79]

All of human history disproves this. In ancient Egypt, Rome, and feudal Europe, the people of property blocked change; change came and could only have come from those with little or no property. Indeed, the whole point of Malthus's book was to help England's people of property *prevent* the sort of improvements to government that were then being driven forward from below in North America and France.

One of the important "improvements" in government that Malthus advocated was to abolish the Poor Laws. As noted above, by 1800 real wages had been driven down to half of what they had been 300 years earlier. But even this was not enough, for there was still a floor below which the workers could not be driven: the Poor Laws. Administered by church parishes, this reform was instituted in 1597 by an English government frightened by years of intense popular unrest.[80] From the moment this social safety net was put in place, real wages rose and continued to do so for the next 150 years, reversing the trend of falling wages that had prevailed over the previous century.[81]

As Malthus complained, the Poor Laws meant that "every man in this country, under certain circumstances, is

entitled by law to parish assistance; and unless his disqual-
ification is clearly proved, has a right to complain if it be
withheld." [82] He acknowledged that this poor relief was not
exactly generous:

> It is known that many almost starving families have been
> found in London and other great towns, who are deterred
> from going on the parish by the crowded, unhealthy and
> horrible state of the workhouses into which they would be
> received, if indeed they could be received at all.[83]

As is often the case, little of the money allocated actually got to the poor. "Some think that the money must be
embezzled for private use; others, that the churchwardens
and overseers consume the greatest part of it in feasting. All
agree that somehow or other it must be very ill managed," a
reality effectively portrayed in Charles Dickens's novel *Oliver
Twist*. As a Church officer, Malthus was in a good position
to know how parish funds were ill managed. But according
to him, the problem was not that this program was badly
administered, but that it existed at all. "The immense sums
distributed to the poor in this country, by the parochial laws,
are improperly called charity. They want its most distin-
guishing attribute," [84] which is that it was not voluntary but
an entitlement; the poor had a right to it. The result, complained Malthus, was that "on the side of givers, instead of
pleasurable sensations, [there was] unceasing discontent and
irritation"—on the side of *givers*!

Even worse, in Malthus's opinion, was its effect on the side
of the receivers. Entitlement social programs tend to break
down divisions among working people and build social soli-
darity. In addition, these programs establish a floor for wages. When employers try to drive wages below the standard
of living offered by a social entitlement program such as the
Poor Laws, welfare, or old-age pensions, toilers do better to

quit working and go on public relief or retire. It provides a small economic sanctuary, a corner into which the toilers can retreat, economically independent from desperate subordination to the employers' whim. It is the modern equivalent of the medieval communal forest, where in hard times dinner could always be found without having to beg or work for the lord.

In addition, this portion of social wealth, which is returned as social programs to the class that produced it, is not available to be pocketed by the wealthy. Abolishing these programs, like restricting the peasants' access to the forest, frees that much more wealth to be appropriated by the ruling class. More important, it throws millions of toilers back onto the job market—just as it forced the poorest and the oldest, and therefore the most desperate peasants under the thumb of the lord—and exerts powerful downward pressure on all wages, from which every single employer benefits.

The social safety net of the Poor Laws, thin and miserly though it was, should be abolished, Malthus argued.[85]

> Among the lower classes, where the point is of the greatest importance, the poor laws afford a direct, constant, and systematical encouragement to marriage, by removing from each individual that heavy responsibility, which he would incur by the laws of nature, for bringing beings into the world which he could not support.[86]

He proposed a rule declaring that "no child born from any marriage taking place after the expiration of a year from the date of the law, and no illegitimate child born two years from the same date, should ever be entitled to parish assistance." *"They must starve."* [87]

Malthus's proposal became law in 1834, when, Engels noted,

> all relief in money and provisions was abolished; the only

relief allowed was admission to the workhouses immediately built. The regulations for these workhouses, or, as the people call them, Poor Law Bastilles [after the notorious French prison torn down during the revolution], is such as to frighten away every one who has the slightest prospect of life without this form of public charity.[88]

The English parliament thereby implemented the ideology "that pauperism is *poverty which the workers have brought upon themselves by their own fault*, and therefore it is not a misfortune which must be prevented, but rather a crime which has to be suppressed and punished," explained Marx.[89]

From their low point in 1801, wages thereafter in England had been on a generally rising trend. Abolishing the Poor Laws jerked the entitlement floor out from under the feet of workers, successfully producing an immediate drop in wages.*[90] It also produced conditions for working people so horrific that a physical stunting of the working class ensued.[91]

But for the rulers, it was the best of times. The unprecedented economic expansion of the decades surrounding 1800 paled compared to the explosive wealth that showered down upon the propertied classes in the 1830s.[92] But the wage decline was temporary, and wages began to rise again in the 1840s with the Chartist movement and the early trade unions.

---

* In a modern parallel, real wages in the US rose steadily from the post–World War II strike wave until 1973. For the next two decades, real wages were driven down, bottoming out in 1993. Faced with renewed upward wage pressure in the early 1990s, the liberal Democratic administration of William Clinton abolished the threadbare and inadequate social net known as welfare, successfully sharpening desperation and competition among working people, putting downward pressure on wages and accelerating the transfer to and concentration of wealth in the richest 10 percent.

DESPOTIC CHARITY

MALTHUS DID BELIEVE THAT, properly administered, there was a useful role for charity, in contrast to entitlement programs like the Poor Laws. The problem under the existing system, he wrote, was that the "sums distributed to the poor in this country" were not raised by voluntary contributions; the Poor Laws were not charity at all but an entitlement. "Essential to voluntary charity," Malthus insisted, was "despotic power," as this "gives the greatest facility to the selection of worthy objects of relief . . . no man should look to charity as a fund on which he may confidently depend." Besides, "one of the most valuable parts of charity is its effect upon the giver."[93]

Malthus put his finger on a basic truth: the purpose of charity is not to help the poor but to help the giver—the propertied classes—control the poor by wielding "despotic power" to pick and choose those (obedient) "worthy objects of relief" and punish rebels with starvation. Voluntary charity also allows the wealthy to feel good about distributing crumbs while pocketing the lion's share of the wealth sheared from the producers. "It is more blessed to give than to receive," Reverend Malthus piously quoted the Bible.[94] Indeed.

MORAL DEFICIENCY, GOD, AND DECEIT

THE WORKING CLASS FAILS to respect the private property and rule of the wealthy not merely for lack of education, according to Malthus, but also because they are morally deficient. "I believe there will be found very few, who pass through the ordeal of squalid and hopeless poverty, or even of long continued embarrassed circumstances, without a considerable moral degradation of character."[95] He continued,

> When indigence does not produce overt acts of vice, it palsies every virtue, . . . the continued temptations which beset hopeless poverty, and the strong sense of injustice that

generally accompanies it from an ignorance of its true cause, tend so powerfully to sour the disposition, to harden the heart, and deaden the moral sense that, generally speaking, virtue takes her flight clear away from the tainted spot, and does not often return.[96]

Malthus did not address the "moral degradation of character" that led people like himself to advocate starving to death foundlings and orphans in order to preserve the "perfect security of property" of the ruling class.

Starvation and government policy were not the only two weapons Malthus advocated to enforce his principle of population. Throughout, Malthus wielded God like a club with which to beat the toilers into submission. Moral restraint was "the proper check to population. . . . The Christian religion places our present as well as future happiness in the exercise of those virtues." [97]

> It is absolutely certain that the *only* mode, consistent with the laws of morality and religion, of giving to the poor the largest share of the property of the rich, without sinking the whole community in misery, is the exercise on the part of the poor of prudence in marriage, and of economy both before and after it. . . . [98] To the Christian I would say that the scriptures most clearly and precisely point it out to us as our duty, to restrain our passions within the bounds of reason; and it is a palpable disobedience of this law to indulge our desires in such a manner, as reason tells us, will unavoidably end in misery. The Christian cannot consider the difficulty of moral restraint as any argument against its being his duty; since in almost every page of the sacred writings . . . [99]

and so on and on and on.

But there was still the problem of the French Revolution.

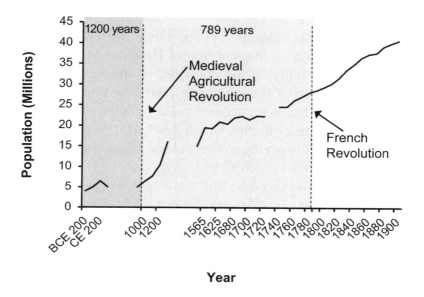

Figure 1 Population of France

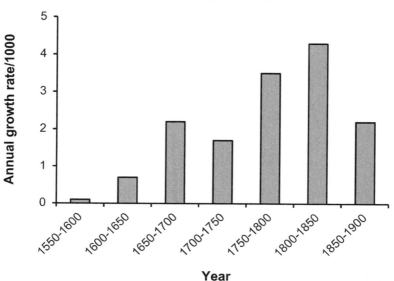

Figure 2 Population growth rate in France

Malthus noted that "the improved condition of the lower classes of people in France since the revolution [has] . . . been much insisted upon." How did Malthus explain this? By applying his doctrine, of course: "The improved condition of the labouring classes in France since the revolution has been accompanied by a greatly diminished proportion of births, which has had its natural and necessary effect in giving to these classes a greater share of the produce of the country." [100]

This was a bald-faced lie; the truth is precisely the opposite. The population of France did not decline, as Malthus claimed, but continued to increase during the period of the 1789 revolution and thereafter (figure 1).[101] As one would expect, the Medieval Agrarian Revolution and the technical advances in agricultural technique that it produced led to an approximate tripling of the population—reflecting a tripling or quadrupling of agricultural production. During the feudal era, the population continued to increase more slowly and erratically, plateauing briefly around 1740. Then from about 1750, population once more began a steady, more continuous increase.

According to the data provided by one devout Malthusite, not only did total population grow during the revolutionary period, but the rate of increase accelerated (figure 2).[102] From 1700 to 1750, the annual rate of increase was about 1.7 per thousand per year. This jumped to an annual rate of 3.5 during the revolutionary period and then soared to 4.3. For rational people, this faster growth is not surprising, as working people were now freer to innovate and less was being squandered on titled layabouts, but it is striking in light of the fact that these included the most intense years of the Napoleonic Wars, when many of France's farmers were off fighting and dying.

Malthus was half right: expropriating France's parasitic feudal elite and abolishing the "perfect security of property" of the nobility did indeed result in surging population among the toilers. This led, however, not to crisis but to an improvement in the condition of the toilers, a revolution in technology, and a higher standard of living for most, though the king and some of the former ruling nobles did come up short.*[103]

And how did this devout worshipper of the status quo and its ruling elite explain the ongoing misery in England, which, by definition, was the best of all possible worlds?** Malthus wrote:

> It is a truth, which I trust has been sufficiently proved in the course of this work, that under a government constructed upon the best and purest principles, and executed by men of the highest talents and integrity, the most squalid poverty and wretchedness might universally prevail from the principle of population alone.[104]

According to Reverend Malthus, even the finest government can do nothing about the laws of God and of nature— the principle of population—which inescapably produce "the most squalid poverty and wretchedness."

---

* This has been true throughout history. The overthrow around 1200 BCE of Mycenaean state slavery in ancient Greece and the establishment of small-farmer democracy produced a tenfold increase in population and a doubling in the standard of living. By 1200 CE, the overthrow of the Roman slaveholder civilization produced explosive population growth, a higher standard of living for the vast majority, and the flowering of a new, higher form of civilization.

** In his novel *Candide*, Voltaire ridiculed slavish supporters of the status quo through the character of the youth Candide, who went out into the world and discovered a harsh and brutal reality, in sharp contrast to what he had been taught by his professor, Dr. Pangloss, that the existing status quo was "the best of all possible worlds."

The Malthusian deceit begins with the title, "An Essay on the Principle of Population." This essay was never intended to apply to the "population" as a whole; the harsh preventive and positive checks that Malthus advocates are aimed exclusively at the workers and rural toilers. For when the monarchs, nobles, capitalists, bankers, and landlords multiply like rabbits, beyond the resources of the society to support them, they do not starve. Nor does Malthus think that they should. On the contrary, more workers and farmers should starve to support them.

REPRESSION

IF GOD, CHARITY, STARVATION, indoctrination, deceit, and his ideology all failed to keep the laboring classes in their place, then Malthus advocated using force. After food shortages in 1800 and 1801, Malthus wrote that, after talking to some

> labouring men, during the late scarcities, I confess that I was to the last degree disheartened at observing their inveterate prejudices on the subject of grain; and I felt very strongly the almost absolute incompatibility of a government really free with such a degree of ignorance. The delusions are of such a nature that, if acted upon, they must at all events be repressed by force.[105]

If the "labouring men" simply could not learn to starve quietly and passively, Malthus argued, dictatorship was in order. "The patriot," he argued, should "submit to very great oppression, rather than give the slightest countenance to a popular tumult." *Vox populi, vox Dei* (the voice of the people is the voice of God) was a Latin saying popular in England at the time. Malthus countered, "if the *vox populi* had been allowed to speak, it would have appeared to be the voice of error and absurdity instead of the *vox Dei*."[106]

PLAGIARISM

MALTHUS'S DOCTRINE ALSO CANNOT be explained as having been so bold and original that it swept otherwise intelligent people off their feet (as it does still today, despite being absurdly inaccurate). In reality, his thesis was a crude plagiarism of numerous writers of his time. Marx pointed out that

> this work in its first form is nothing more than a school-boyish, superficial plagiarism of Defoe, Sir James Steuart, Townsend, Franklin, Wallace, etc., declaimed in the manner of a sermon, but not containing a single original proposition of Malthus himself. The great sensation this pamphlet caused was due solely to the fact that it corresponded to the interests of a particular party. The French Revolution had found passionate defenders in the United Kingdom; the "principle of population", slowly worked out in the eighteenth century, and then, in the midst of a great social crisis, proclaimed with drums and trumpets as the infallible antidote to the doctrines of Condorcet, etc., was greeted jubilantly by the English oligarchy as the great destroyer of all hankerings after a progressive development of humanity.[107]

Even Malthus's claim that population increases geometrically, doubling every thirty years, was lifted from the Italian economist Giammaria Ortes.[108]

Apparently, Marx was not the first to notice Malthus's plagiarism. In the preface to the first edition of his book, Malthus pretended that his work was original, claiming that "as the subject opened upon [the author], some ideas occurred, which he did not recollect to have met with before." In the second edition, the preface was altered to acknowledge some of the sources from whom Malthus stole: "The only authors from whose writings I had deduced the principle, which formed the main argument of the essay, were Hume,

Wallace, Dr. Adam Smith, and Dr. Price." [109]

Even this correction is false. Later in this same revised preface, Malthus claimed that "in the course of this inquiry I found that much more had been done than I had been aware of, when I first published the essay." Only then did he mention Townsend and others, but did not acknowledge them as the source of his ideas, and he still did not credit Anderson. Another pastor, Johann Peter Süssmilch, published a book along similar lines some fifty years earlier, *The Divine Order in the Changes of the Human Race as Shown by its Birth, Death, and Propagation*. Malthus clearly knew and used Süssmilch's book, as he cited tables from it, but he did not acknowledge in his preface having gotten any ideas from him. [110]

SURPLUS POPULATION AND CAPITALISM

ALTHOUGH MALTHUS MAY HAVE been a master theologian-propagandist-apologist-plagiarist for the ruling elite, he understood little about the workings of the system he was defending. His dogma claims that surplus population, with its attendant unemployment and poverty, is caused by the poor having too many babies. This is false.

When production is expanding, the capitalists need millions of workers—the reserve army of unemployed labor—available and ready to step up to the machines immediately to produce at break-neck pace the many commodities the bosses hope to sell at a profit as each capitalist competes with every other to exploit the market opportunities—while they last. In such times of expansion, the chaos of capitalist competition leads all capitalists to pursue the same market opportunities to excess, leading inevitably within a decade to a crisis of overproduction: more is produced than can be sold. Sales fall, production slows, and the economy turns downward.

Suddenly, these same millions of workers who yesterday were essential, today are surplus. This is not because a surplus number of babies was born the day before the downturn, as Malthus pretends, but because of the lawful, chaotic functioning of the capitalist system. Unemployment results from such crises of overproduction; by the end of a war among capitalist powers, producing a collapse of war production; or it occurs when capitalists have sucked a semicolonial country dry and its economy disintegrates, as occurs regularly today. Thus, unemployment follows from these or any number of other reasons over which workers have absolutely no control.

But according to Malthusian ideology, this new condition of being unemployed is entirely the fault of the workers themselves. Yesterday these toilers were essential to the production of capitalist profits. Today they and the parents who bore them are sinners and criminals, having contravened the will of God, the law of nature, and the good of the nation by continuing to exist when their labor power is no longer needed. The penalty for their crime against God and nation, according to Malthus, should be to starve to death.

And what happens when the economy again comes out of one of these regular troughs? The manufacturers cannot wait for a new generation of laborers to be born and come of age; an army of unemployed must be standing in reserve, ready to step up to the machine at a moment's notice. Malthus's ignorance of the basic needs of the capitalist economy is as vast as the dishonesty of his solutions.

But when production and profits are rising, unemployment falls and workers naturally organize to fight for a greater share of the wealth they produce. This fact, combined with competition among capitalists, drives the latter to replace workers with "labor-saving" machines.[111] If the manufacturer can install a new machine with which six workers can produce what ten did before, then the remaining four become surplus and are laid off. Following

Malthus's prescript and reducing the number of surplus workers would put upward pressure on wages and accelerate the search for labor-saving machinery—and the pace at which workers would be made redundant.[112]

Capitalist profits are expanded by working some to death fourteen to sixteen hours a day while others stand idle and starve.[113] Even during periods of peak production, the capitalists prefer there still be a pool of unemployed, because this puts downward pressure on the wages of those who are working. If production picks up to the point that most of the reserve industrial army of unemployed finds jobs and therefore begins to disappear, the ability of bosses to pit employed against unemployed is weakened and wages tend to rise. Thus, unemployment and poverty are not caused by the working class having too many babies; it is the natural functioning of the capitalist economy that creates the reserve army of unemployed *and is utterly dependent on it.*[114]

From 1551 to 1600, a boy who reached the age of fifteen would live on average to age fifty-seven, a girl to thirty-eight.[115] If they tried to obey the laws of God and nature as preached by Reverend Malthus, waiting until age thirty or later before having children, they would succeed only in producing more, not fewer, hungry orphans, because they would probably be dead before their children were grown. If one really tried to follow the zigs and zags of the absurdities in the Malthus doctrine to their logical conclusions, one would have to conclude that no worker should ever bear a child until after first acquiring a notarized document from a capitalist guaranteeing lifetime employment to this yet-to-be-born worker. But just stating this requirement exposes its idiocy; no capitalist would ever issue such a guarantee, for one of the most sacred "freedoms" that all capitalists cling to under "free enterprise" is the right to toss surplus workers into the gutter on a moment's notice to protect their profits.

WHAT IT LEAVES OUT

FOR ALL THE DECEITS and absurdities in Malthus's ideology, its most serious flaw "lies not in what it maintains, but in what it ignores":[116] the property and class relations within which population grows and contracts.

The Jew-hater can always find one greedy Jew to whom he points as proof of his thesis; the racist can find one lazy or violent person of color. The deceit lies in the claim that these attributes are typical of and limited to these groups and are responsible for the ills of society. Appealing to racism or antisemitism diverts the toilers' attention from the fact that greed, idleness, and violence are in fact most concentrated in the ruling class and are inherent to the class societies they defend. In times of crisis, when the rage of the exploited boils over, the rulers deflect that anger onto these handy scapegoats, whom they happily sacrifice in defense of their privileges.

The narrowness of vision that Malthus demands is different, however, for there is not a single historical example that upholds his doctrine. Let's look at a typical, modern example of the real reasons for crises under capitalism. Capitalist governments today restrict food production and subsidize the profits of the biggest food corporations. These freeby programs and competition among imperialist powers for the world food trade force farmers in semicolonial countries out of business, opening new markets for major agricultural corporations based in imperialist countries. Farmers in Latin America are threatened by the ax of US–imposed "free trade" agreements.[117]

Rice is the main food source in large parts of the world, including Haiti. Rice is also the most heavily subsidized of all US crops; three of the top five welfare recipients are primarily rice distributors. The largest in 2004, Arkansas-based Riceland Foods, raked in over half a billion dollars in government profit give-aways from 1995 to 2004.[118] In 1994, US President William Clinton—from Arkansas—sent troops to occupy Haiti. Before the invasion, Haiti produced 95 percent of its own rice. As one of the spoils of conquest, Clinton forced Haiti to eliminate tariffs protecting small Haitian rice farmers. US government handouts enabled corporate exporters to dump rice on the Haitian market at below cost and wipe out local production. Now Haiti is forced to import its rice—80 percent of it from the US, and much of this from the Clintons' corporate backers in Arkansas.

For all the deceits and absurdities in Malthus's ideology, its most serious flaw lies not in what it maintains, but in what it ignores

This allowed capitalists to double the price of rice in Haiti in the first six months of 2004 alone. Driven out of business, former rice farmers crowded into Haiti's cities looking for work. Food prices rose beyond the reach of much of Haiti's population, producing riots by 2008. In 2009, the Haitian parliament passed a bill proposing to raise the minimum wage from twenty-four to sixty-one cents an hour; garment manufacturers, including for the Hanes and Levi Strauss corporations, were furious. US President Barack Obama's State Department was headed by Hillary Clinton, and William Clinton was deputized by the UN as a "special envoy" to Haiti to assist in this second assault.

US State Department officials in Haiti spoke out repeatedly against the wage increase, applying pressure. After a campaign of several months, Haiti's president was strong-armed into blocking even this meager wage raise, holding the poorest of the poor on the knife's edge of survival, where any disruption guaranteed catastrophe. In 2010, an earthquake wiped out many of these low-paying jobs. The Clintons had already eliminated the farmers, and the Obama administration helped keep wages below subsistence level, so the Haitians now had no way to either pay for imported rice or grow their own; starvation ensued. Many Haitians took to eating mud cakes and straw,[119] while Riceland Foods sales soared to over a billion dollars a year, with a profit margin of nearly 60 percent.[120] Mission accomplished.

A pious Malthusian would survey this devastation, meticulously count the number of mouths and the amount of food available, and proclaim that Malthus was right: the population exceeded the food supply; it was their own fault. This conclusion is mathematically precise and breathtakingly dishonest. Such pinhole tunnel vision is necessary to make the Malthus theory work and good propaganda for concealing the real causes. Engels explained, "not enough is being produced, that is the root of the whole problem. But *why* is not enough being produced? Not because the limits of production have been reached. . . . No, but because the limits of production are determined not by the number of hungry bellies, but rather by the number of purchasers with full *purses*." "It is to the everlasting disgrace of modern bourgeois development that it has not yet progressed beyond the economic forms of the animal kingdom."[121] Haiti is indeed one of the most densely populated countries in the world; but the Netherlands is even more densely populated, and it exports surplus food.

The examples in Germany in the 1500s and in Haiti in 2010 illustrate that famines do not just happen; they are created by the existing class relations.* Understanding how requires looking at the political and economic context. Famines are the natural consequence of economic systems where, as Adam Smith pointed out, "all for ourselves and nothing for other people, seems, in every age of the world, to have been the vile maxim of the masters of mankind."[122] And again, contrary to Malthus's theology, these laws are not immutable. They can be overturned by revolution, as they have

---

* On famines in Germany, see Dees, *Power of Peasants*, esp. chap. 10.

been repeatedly, with the overthrow of Rome in 476 and the Medieval Agricultural Revolution around the year 1000, the overthrow of feudalism in the 1500s–1600s in England and Holland, and in 1776 and 1789 in the United States and France. In every case, revolutions in social relations led to advances in agricultural technique that allowed the population to soar through the old "population ceilings."

IDEOLOGY, NOT THEORY

THIS IS THE MALTHUSIAN IDEOLOGY: dishonesty, plagiarism, greed, mysticism, theology, brutality, despotism, and contempt for the working majority, and yet still today, "most discussions of historical demography start, continue, and finish" with Malthus.[123]

Famines do not just happen; they are created

In the early 1600s, Galileo pointed out that that the Earth is not the immobile center of the universe; it circles the Sun. His break with mysticism and Aristotle's slaveholder ideology, his use of the scientific method to understand and explain our physical world, rightly won Galileo the title of father of modern science. But even Galileo made mistakes. His initial theory on the cause of tides, for example, was wrong. The tides are not caused by the combined effects of the Earth's rotating on its axis and circling the Sun but by the gravitational pull of the Moon. At the core of Galileo's explanation was an honest attempt, based on evidence available at the time, to advance our understanding of the world. But scientific theories must be supported by facts or they are scrapped. As a result, the lineage of the modern scientific view of the rotation of the planets still today is traced through Galileo, but his explanation of the tides, despite its illustrious paternity, has no adherents—it has been proven wrong and therefore discarded.

However, the fact that there is not a single historical example that validates Malthus's doctrine and that every historical experience refutes it has had no effect on its success. This ideology has only gained supporters over time, as the gap between its predictions and reality has grown. This is because it was never a scientific theory, but a religious-political ideology. It was never an honest attempt, based on the evidence available at the time, to advance understanding of our world. From its inception, a deliberate deceit was at its core. In this, Malthusianism is more akin to antisemitism and racism. These three ideologies are never affected by attempts to disprove them scientifically because they were never based on fact to start with. They survive and even flourish because of their *usefulness* to the interests of the ruling elite. At the heart of each is an attempt to preserve the status quo by concealing the root cause of problems in society and diverting blame for them away from the ruling class and onto scapegoats.

Malthusianism is more akin to antisemitism and racism

Since the rise of class society, ideologues and theologians have followed Plato's method of personal dishonesty by inventing "noble lies" to rationalize the rule of the few over the many. Malthus's ideology is nothing more than a repackaging of the age-old fable that the suffering of the poor is God's punishment for their own sinfulness.

But times had changed. Malthus lived during the French Revolution—the first in history fought not behind religious veils, but openly for class interests using the power of the scientific revolution that Galileo had helped reignite. Like Aristotle and Aquinas before him, Reverend Malthus understood that religious rationalizations for maintaining class hierarchy were losing their grip. So Malthus made two additions. He specified which sin God was punishing the poor for: having too many babies. And he supplied the (plagia-rized) formula that always and everywhere food supplies grow arithmetically while population grows geometrical-ly—oh so mathematical and scientific-sounding, but utterly fraudulent and easily disproved.

Although Reverend Malthus's modern acolytes pass over in silence the central role of religion in the Malthusian doc-trine, ignoring the mystical core of this ideology does not make it more scientific. Saint Thomas Malthus lives on in the pantheon of the immortals for those who continue to wield religion and ignoble lies as weapons of social control, as he does for those who today conceal the religious core of the Malthusian doctrine in an attempt to prolong the usefulness of this mumbo-jumbo. Apologists for the status quo still need this deceit, for the alternative is to recognize that for at least the last thousand years, famines have been caused not by nature nor by God but by humans, by the rul-ing elite's greed and lust for power.

MALTHUS TODAY

SOME HISTORIANS CLAIM THAT the economic takeoff of the early medieval period was caused not by the rev-olution in social and property relations but by population growth. This raises the question of why, after 10,000 years, population began growing to such an extent only then; did people suddenly want more sex? These same historians then turn around and claim that this exact same population growth was responsible for the economic stagnation and de-cline of the post-1250 period and fail to see the contradiction between these two positions.[124] This Malthusian population explanation for the ups and downs in the economy never corresponds with the facts but serves well to rob the farmers of credit for the upturn and to divert blame for the downturn from the ruling class onto the common people.

The problem has never been keeping "the population from pressing too hard against the limits of the means of subsistence,"[125] but precisely the opposite: keeping the flood of food from pressing too hard against the rulers' profits. Some writers, recognizing the difficulty of hustling the Malthusian doctrine in the modern world, have tried to salvage Malthus's ideology by claiming that whereas it lost its applicability with the advent of the "technological revolution" of the 1700s and 1800s, it still applies to the medieval era. In an article dramatically titled "Malthus Was Right!," Democratic Party propagandist and *New York Times* columnist Paul Krugman proclaimed, "Malthus was right about *the whole of human history up until his own era*."[126] "The Malthusian model is an accurate description of all societies before 1800," wrote Professor Clark.[127] Others have argued that

> the truth of Malthus' and Ricardo's pessimistic theories is clearly reflected in the facts. . . . It was only really in the nineteenth century that the Malthusian problem was resolved—when, thanks to different forms of progress, especially technological—production was able to keep pace with, or even to keep ahead of, population growth instead of struggling painfully behind.[128]

Another wrote that "we are on the verge of entering a post-Malthusian world."[129]

But as Malthus himself made clear, his book was a response to the American and French Revolutions. His core thesis was that revolution and the technological advances that flow from changed social and property relations *cannot* affect his principle of population, which he maintained is a law of God and of nature, as immutable as the law of gravity. The growing surplus of food that became impossible to conceal in the 1800s did not show that Malthus's thesis was valid up to that point, but no farther. It proved that his core argument—that a revolution in social relations could have no effect on these "laws" of nature and of God—was dead wrong. The attempt to salvage Malthus conceals the fact that the technological revolution of the 1800s was the result of prior revolutions in social and property relations. Social revolutions and the resulting technological advances made all the difference, disproving *all* of Malthus's dogma.

For at least the last thousand years, famines have been caused not by nature nor by God but by humans, by the ruling elite's greed and lust for power

"Before the mid-eighteenth century English population seemed to have a natural ceiling of around 5.5 million people," yet another historian declared.[130] In reality, England has had several population "ceilings," each of which depended not on nature, as the historian and Malthus claimed, nor on God, as Malthus claimed, but on existing social and property relations and the level of technology. Between the years 100 and 800, the population ceiling of England appears to have been around one million, which it bumped up against more than once.[131] The Medieval Agricultural Revolution shattered that ceiling and allowed the population to soar to a new one of 3.75 million before collapsing in the mid-1300s. England's population reached this level again by 1500, when another social revolution, overturning feudal rule, allowed the farmers to produce enough food to blast through that ceiling. With a brief pause during the civil war of the mid-1600s, it has continued to rise ever since. Today it is over 67 million.[132]

Through revolution, working farmers overcame the old forms of social control and won enough personal and economic freedom to engage in experimentation; technical progress followed. But, as was the case with the Medieval Agricultural

Revolution, it was the changing social relations that preceded and made possible the technological revolution, not the reverse. A similar trend can be traced for France (figure 1).

This leaves the question of whether it is true, as several historians maintain, that amid the wreckage of Malthus's failed ideology, some shard can be found that still applies to the feudal era. There is not. It has long been shown that at the latest after 1500, famines in England were caused by the pursuit of profit despite an adequate food supply.[133] Those who were there and lived through famines in England in the 1500s and 1600s reported that "last yeares famin was made by man and not by God," and "evill disposed persons . . . without pity towards poore men, by their engrossing [hoarding] of grayne and other abuses will make want amidst plentifulness."[134] Thomas More pointed out in the early 1500s that "if you'd inspected every rich man's barn, . . . everyone could so easily get enough to eat."[135] This was true not solely in England. It also held in Germany and the rest of feudal Europe.

In one of the most prominent texts today on the German Peasant War of 1525, Professor David Sabean claimed "Two primary factors lay behind the situation that led to the revolt. The first was a sharp and continuing rise in population. Secondly was the ecological factor: the geography of the region precluded splitting up farms into ever smaller units."[136] He argued that the Peasant War was more about farmers fighting each other than about the class conflict between farmers and the lord, whom he fawningly alleged was "solicitous for all his subjects,"[137] though he provided not a shred of evidence to support this flattery. Not surprisingly, this is the same professor who made his name claiming that rents were not rising prior to the Peasant War, when his own data showed precisely the opposite. But he got Malthus's methodology right, including neglecting to mention his source. Note also that this is the same argument used by witch hunt historians: "Their social goals arose out of inner-village antagonisms."* [138]

The reach of these findings goes even further. "The transformation of the eighteenth and nineteenth centuries had an even longer genesis than has been thought, since almost all the technological innovations [in agriculture] that brought it about can be found as far back as the thirteenth century." [139] Thus, the takeoff in English agriculture after 1500 took place—using technology that was then centuries old—because of changing social and property relations. The Industrial Revolution of the 1700s and 1800s only added momentum to a process already well under way.

Even during famine years in the early 1570s, the farmers of south Germany produced twice as much food as was needed to feed all of society, and yet thousands starved. Grain production in 2004 reached a historic record, but thanks to the food policies of all the imperialist countries—aimed at reducing production at home and destroying the productive capacity of their competitors—world hunger was rising. [140]

In 2019, American farmers worked sixteen to eighteen hours a day and were "producing more grain and food than the world market can absorb," according to the *New York Times*, but often were paid less than production costs for their crops. [141] And yet, due to the success of US government policies, subsidized profits for the major agricultural corporations were high while some 800 million people in the world were starving. [142] The *New York Times* article concluded, "American farmers are victims of their own success." [143] Classic Malthus dogma: it's their own damn fault.

The ideological objective, from Plato to Malthus, has always been to make people believe that the cause of this human misery and the obstacle to progress are the poor them-

---

* See Dees, *Power of Peasants*, chap. 14, "Flat rents and declining serfdom," and "Witch hunts" in chap. 9, "Control."

selves. The solution, Malthus asserted, is not revolution but the maze-with-no-exit of population control. The purpose of Malthus's essay, as Marx pointed out, was "to provide 'economic' proof, in the interests of the *existing* English government and the *landed aristocracy*, that the tendency of the French Revolution and *its adherents in England* to perfect matters was utopian."[144] Counterposed to Malthus's claims that food supply necessarily rises more slowly than population—and that high population must cause starvation—is the scientific view, expressed in 1650 by the English yeoman farmer and captain in the Parliamentary army Walter Blith, that "any land by cost and charge may be made rich, and as rich as land can be,"[145] and again in 1843 by the twenty-three-year-old Engels: "The productive power at humanity's disposal is immeasurable. The productivity of the soil can be increased infinitely by the application of capital, labour and science."[146] This observation is easy to prove. The Netherlands has a population density more than eleven times that of Congo (DRC). According to the Malthus fraud, the people of the Netherlands must be starving, and those of Congo prospering. As with all things Malthusian, the truth is precisely the opposite: it is in Congo where people go hungry, while the crowded Netherlands feeds not only all of its own people but in 2020 was the world's second largest food exporter after the US.[147]

In the years after the explosive success of the first edition of his book in 1798, Malthus traveled widely, collecting data for subsequent editions. But in the course of his assiduous research, he managed to ignore the actual growth of population and food supply in every country he visited, including his native England, where the development of population and agricultural output, during his time and for centuries prior, flatly disproved his thesis. This was taking place not in some distant past or place, but right before Malthus's eyes; Malthus, therefore, wisely chose not to cite England in support of his thesis that the growth of the population always outstrips that of the food supply.

He pointed instead to what was then a faraway and little-known backwater, the United States, so that few of his readers would be able to test his claims against personal experience. He alleged that in the US, "the population was found to double itself for some successive periods every twenty-five years." Far from believing this to be an extraordinary example, he wrote, "I have undoubtedly taken the increase of population smaller, and the increase of produce greater, than they really would be." He argued that "no probable reason can be assigned, why the population should not double itself in less, if possible, than fifteen years." Malthus claimed that his formula for population growth was "incontrovertible," [148] and far from exaggerating, his formula understated actual population growth.

The crowded Netherlands feeds not only all of its own people but is the world's second largest food exporter after the US

It is very easy to test his claim. Figure 3 shows the population in the US in 1790, the actual increase, and what it should have been in 2015 based on Malthus's formula of doubling every 25 years. [149] The population of the US in 1790 was about 3.93 million people; in 2015 it was 321.36 million. According to Malthus's formula, it should have been over two billion.

This alone is a fatal error in his dogma, but only the first of many. Actually, the numbers in figure 3 show Malthus's prediction of what the population would have been if not a single immigrant had entered the country after 1790; but the *Reality* line includes everyone, so the real gap between dogma and truth is far greater, as adding in the millions of immigrants who flooded US shores and their offspring would only widen the abyss of Malthus's blunder. Similarly

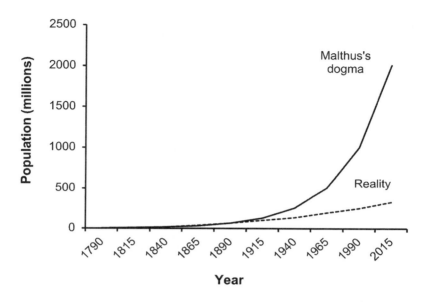

Figure 3 US projected and actual population

in England, in the three centuries before Malthus published his text, population rose between 1520 and 1791 from about 2.4 to 7.74 million—an increase of 3.23 times.[150] According to Malthus's "incontrovertible" formula, the population should have increased more than 1,000 times over to 2.48 billion.

Malthus alleged that this geometric population growth would occur if not checked by what he called "positive checks," by which he meant the mass slaughter of humanity by war, famine, and disease, or "preventive checks," his code for sexual repression. The US is the perfect test case for Malthus's doctrine because (except for the Indians of course) this country has never suffered mass exterminations of significant proportions as a result of war, famine, or disease—Malthus's "positive checks." And although US politicians and preachers to this day have zealously hustled the "preventive check"— sexual repression (for the peons, not for themselves)—it has had little real effect on population growth because US families tended to be large until the second half of the twentieth century. At that point, fewer children per family came not as a result of successful sexual repression or the catastrophes Malthus insisted were necessary, but from the higher standard of living for the working class and *greater* sexual freedom that birth control permitted.

US population growth, although not remotely approaching Malthus's idiotic prediction, has been relatively rapid by any realistic historical experience. Nevertheless, the "problem" throughout most of US history has been not too many but too few people for the needs of the expanding economy. The owners of US industry, through their government, have made up this shortage by allowing a constant stream, at times flood, of immigration, calibrated to provide adequate labor to maximize their profits while maintaining a pool of unemployed to keep downward pressure on wages. So this half of Malthus's "law"— that the population increases geometrically and naturally outstrips the food supply—is ludicrously inaccurate.

What about the food supply? The error in Malthus's prediction on the growth of the food supply is even greater than his prediction on population growth. In fact, the US government has always had the opposite problem. It is not the population that outstripped the food supply, but the food supply that outstripped the population. The increase in agricultural productivity in the US has been so great that, although all but about 1 percent of the population has been driven off the land over the last two centuries, and despite massive government payments to discourage farmers from growing food, the country's food supply is about 50 percent greater than the population's needs.[151] Just in the past half century, although the number of farms has fallen by two-thirds, farm production in the US doubled, outstripping population growth, as always, despite Malthus's prediction.[152] In 2005, the huge harvest in corn overwhelmed the available storage facilities, and mountains of corn piled up outside full elevators, "with corn spilling out everywhere," as one article put it. The harvest the year before was even larger.[153] The oversupply of food so exceeds the population that it is a threat to capitalist profits.

Peasants in the early 1200s noted that the rulers would seek to profit from "even the air" if they could.[154] What stops feudal and capitalist exploiters from profiteering from the air is that the supply is too great and cannot be controlled. They face almost the same problem today with food. With the application of capital and technology, it can be grown anywhere in almost boundless quantity. The average US farmer now produces enough to feed 155 people,[155] and this number no doubt could be raised much higher. With the application of capital and technology, every farmer on the planet could produce food in these quantities. If this were to occur, however, food would be as plentiful as air and sunlight, and it would be just as impossible for a handful of capitalists to profiteer from it.

The response of the US government to the threat to capitalist profits of an oversupply of food has been to reduce the abundance by paying farmers to take land out of production,*[156] and to destroy the productive capacity of competing food producers. This is accomplished by subsidizing primarily the largest US food corporations, currently to the tune of about $19 billion every year. In the US in 2005, the top 1 percent of these recipients raked in 20 percent of total payments; 20 percent of them amassed 83 percent of the giveaways. In 2000, the total reached $22.7 billion, which 2005, with its huge bumper crop, nearly matched. Two-thirds of US farmers and ranchers receive no support, and of those who do, the bottom 80 percent received an average of $704 each per year from 1995 to 2005.[157]

Thus, the relatively small payments that some family farmers receive under this program seek to buy their compliance for this program specifically and for the economic

---

* In 2007, a US government program paid out $1.8 billion to some 400,000 farmers for idling 36.8 million acres of land—an area greater than that of New York State.

system generally, but actually only keep them on the brink of survival (at best) and widen the gulf between them and the major food corporations that dominate them. These hand-outs also increase the cost of land and the amount of ground-rent the farmers have to pay, so what little help the farmers get from these payments is then taken from them in the form of higher mortgages or rents. Finally, it accomplishes the same outcome for farmers as charity does for workers. It allows farmers who are actually losing money or otherwise would be to stay in business, slaving away to produce food that they then sell at below the real cost of production to big agribusinesses, thereby reducing the latter's costs and increasing their profits. The program both directly and indirectly benefits primarily the bankers, large landowners, and big traders.[158]

The farm subsidy program is one of many government-organized transfers of wealth to the wealthy, but it is one with a strategic objective. These massive handouts allow the largest producers to dump food on the world market at well below production costs, thereby undercutting and, its backers hope, eliminating their competitors, be they small rice farmers in Haiti, corn farmers in Mexico, or competing agricultural corporations from other countries. This explains why, despite the pretense of bewilderment from politicians and pundits, these subsidies rise precisely in years of bumper crops,[159] because large crops exacerbate the "problem"—to capitalist profits—of excess supply. The policy reduces the number of growers and increases the largest agricultural corporations' control over the supply. Its effect has been and will continue to be to increase hunger in the world, which in turn drives up the price of food and the income of those dominating the supply. While the corporate profits produced by these government subsidy schemes grow, the token amounts that the US government contributes to programs aimed at increasing food self-sufficiency in semicolonial countries is being slashed.[160] The real policy objective is to increase the world's dependency on US food corporations.

The problem for those corporations, however, is that their main competitors are doing the same thing. The Japanese and Canadian governments fund at a rate even higher than that of the US, and the European Union hands out at least $51 billion a year in agricultural freebies.[161] The thirty OECD governments distributed an estimated $279 billion in subsidies in 2004 alone, up more than 8 percent over the previous year.[162] Trade talks aimed at getting the other side to reduce its giveaways result in one round after another of failure, so the main imperialist countries continue to hold each other in stalemate.

This welfare program for the rich by the imperialist governments also promotes coca and poppy production—from which cocaine and heroin are produced—as small farmers in semicolonial countries, devastated by the crossfire of competition among the imperialist countries, are forced to turn to the only crops they can sell. This ensures a steady supply of these crops for the drug capitalists in one of the most profitable commodity markets in the world today.

In France, the top 25 percent of handout recipients take in about 70 percent of the payments. The fabulously wealthy prince of Monaco is one of the biggest welfare queens. The largest beneficiary in 2004 was—a rice producer. The bottom fifty percent divide roughly 10 percent of the total among themselves.[163]

It is the same in England, where the largest handout beneficiary was the sugar company Tate & Lyle, which received nearly £120 million, or $227 million, in 2004. The company announced pretax profits that year of $429 million. The duke of Buccleuch, who owns much of Scotland, took in £700,000 in government giveaways; the queen raked in £546,000 and Prince (now King) Charles Windsor received £224,000 on the public dole. The duke of Westminster, who owns major chunks of prime real estate in downtown London, got an extra £448,472 in profit supports. And these are just a few examples.[164]

ુ

APPROPRIATELY FOR A PASTOR, Reverend Malthus closed his book with what is more a fervent prayer than a political analysis, which returned to the central issue of his propaganda tract:

> The structure of society, in its great features, will probably always remain unchanged. We have every reason to believe that it will always consist of a class of proprietors and a class of labourers.[165]

The pipedream of immobile history remains an attempt to counter the reality, summarized by Marx and Engels, that "the history of all hitherto existing society is the history of class struggles"[166] and that through class struggle, revolutions have been and can be made that advance the interests of the class of laborers. The fear of the propertied classes of having their great estates divided among us has only grown since Malthus's time. And so, still today, they and their propagandists continue to rock in place on the old hobbyhorse of the pharaohs, Plato, Aristotle, Gregory, Augustine, Aquinas, Luther, Urban, and Malthus, going nowhere, fervently praying that history will do likewise.

Endnotes

1. Floud, "Economics," 241.
2. See for example Blickle, *Revolution of 1525*, 72; Brenner, "Agrarian Class Structure," 14, 18, 61, and "Agrarian Roots," 224–26; Campbell, "Agricultural Progress," 26, with cites to numerous others in this vein; Clark, *Farewell*; Henning, *Handbuch*, 1:729; Herlihy, *Black Death*, 31, 38–39, 81; Hippel, "Bevölkerung," 434; Kießling, Konersmann, and Troßbach, in Kießling and others, *Grundzüge*, 11–18, 259; Le Roy Ladurie in Le Roy Ladurie and Goy, *Tithe and agrarian history*, 191–92; Le Roy Ladurie, "Reply," 101; Livi-Bacci, *Population and Nutrition*, 14–15; Lütge, "Die wirtschaftliche Lage," 338; North and Thomas, *Rise*, 51, 102–05; Pfister, *Bevölkerungsgeschichte*; Rösener, "Agrarian Economy," 72; Schofield, "Impact," 72; Sabean, "German Agrarian Institutions," 76–88; Sabean, *Landbesitz*, 20, 24, 25, 28–36; Sabean, "Social Background," esp. 5, 6, 37, 44, 45, 50–61; Scheidel, "Approaching," 11; Sreenivasan, *Peasants*, esp. 110–114; Wade, *Troublesome Inheritance*, 11; Warde, *Ecology*, 354; Wrigley and Schofield, *Population History*, esp. 459 and following.
3. Scheidel, "Approaching," 11, 13; Temin, "Contribution," 45–70; Herlihy, *Black Death*, 81; Rosenstein, *Rome at War*.
4. Cipolla, *Before*, 136; similarly; See Herlihy, *Black Death*, 31, 38–39, 81; and Rösener, *Peasants*, 33–34.
5. Clark, *Farewell*, 5, 27, 101–02,

259. Similarly, see Wade, *Troublesome Inheritance*, 161.

6. Rosenstein, *Rome at War*, 155, 167.

7. Henning, *Handbuch*, 1:729.

8. Pfister, *Bevölkerungsgeschichte*, 12. See also Hippel, "Bevölkerung," 434.

9. Fogel, "Relevance of Malthus," 1, 2. The Organisation for Economic Co-operation and Development (OECD) historically included the imperialist countries of Europe, North America, and the Pacific. In recent years, a few semicolonial states have been admitted.

10. See for example Mydans, "Resisting Birth Control"; Rosenthal, "Nigeria's Population"; Wines, "Malnutrition."

11. Cowell, "Demographic Time Bomb."

12. See for example Abel, *Agricultural Fluctuations*, 3, 41, 45 and following, 146, 296. See also Abel, *Die Wüstungen*; and Pfister, *Bevölkerungsgeschichte*.

13. Marx, "Theories of Surplus Value," 31:348.

14. Kautsky, *Der Einfluss*, 6.

15. Quoted in Thompson, *Making*, 57.

16. Murphy, *History*, 424, 441, 455, 483.

17. Crouzet, "Toward an Export Economy," 78.

18. Real wages appear to have fallen to about 55 percent in 1800 from their peak in the 1400s according to Allen, "Great Divergence," 434, fig. 10. Real wages were about 35 percent of what they had been in 1500, and less than 31 percent of what they had been at their peak in 1477 according to the wage series in Wrigley and Schofield, *Population History*, Appendix 9, 638–41; and Phelps Brown and Hopkins, "Seven Centuries," Appendix B, 311–14.

19. Quoted in Hobsbawm, *Industry and Empire*, 95.

20. Edgcumbe, *Diary*, 8.

21. Quoted in Thompson, *Making*, 56.

22. Thompson, *Making*, 57, 104.

23. Malthus, *Essay* (1803), 75.

24. Malthus, *Essay* (1803), 247.

25. Hobsbawm, *Industry and Empire*, 95, quotes at 77, 94.

26. Philp, *Godwin's Political Justice*, 58–59.

27. Malthus, *Essay* (1798), 287. This edition reproduces the 1798 first edition. The argument in this text draws on both editions.

28. Malthus, *Essay* (1798), i.

29. On the impact of Godwin's polemics in England at the time, see Salt's introduction to Godwin, *Political Justice*, 1–32.

30. Wollstonecraft, *Love Letters*, xii–xiii, xvi–xvii, xxiv.

31. Hansen, *Too Many Babies?*, 12.

32. Malthus, *Essay* (1803), 247–48.

33. Godwin, quoted in Malthus, *Essay* (1798), 177–78.

34. Malthus, *Essay* (1798), 266–67.

35. See chap. 4, "Rise of the papacy."

36. Marx, "Contribution to the Critique of Political Economy," 263.

37. Marx, "Thesen über Feuerbach," 533; mistranslated in "Theses on Feuerbach," 7.

38. Malthus, *Essay* (1803), 179, 263, 278.
39. Malthus, *Essay* (1803), 329.
40. Malthus, *Essay* (1798), 204 (emphasis added), 291.
41. Malthus, *Essay* (1803), 263.
42. Quoted in James, *Population Malthus*, 43.
43. Malthus, *Essay* (1803), 252.
44. Malthus, *Essay* (1803), 21, quote on 225; see also 23, 215.
45. Malthus, *Essay* (1803), 223.
46. Malthus, *Essay* (1803), 218, see also 219.
47. Malthus, *Essay* (1803), 24, 238–39.
48. Plato, "Laws" 841.
49. Malthus, *Essay* (1803), 22.
50. Malthus, *Essay* (1803), 262.
51. Malthus, *Essay* (1803), 226.
52. Malthus, *Essay* (1803), 249 (emphasis in original), 264.
53. Williams, "Original Anti-Vaxxers."
54. Malthus, *Essay* (1803), 240.
55. Malthus, *Essay* (1803), 237.
56. Malthus, *Essay* (1803), 209.
57. Malthus, *Essay* (1803), 236–37 (emphasis added).
58. Malthus, *Essay* (1803), 75.
59. Malthus, *Essay* (1803), 76.
60. Malthus, *Essay* (1803), 78.
61. Arthur Young, quoted in Malthus, *Essay* (1803), 293; see 293 and following; 289.
62. Malthus, *Essay* (1803), 86.
63. Malthus, *Essay* (1803), 101.
64. Allen, "Tracking," 217; Allen, "Great Divergence," 434, fig. 10.
65. Malthus, *Essay* (1803), 119; Marx, "Trades' Unions."
66. Malthus, *Essay* (1803), 72, 253.
67. Malthus, *Essay* (1803), 65 (emphasis added).
68. Malthus, *Essay* (1803), 24, 218, 368–69.
69. Malthus, *Essay* (1803), 276.
70. Malthus, *Essay* (1803), 227.
71. North, *Structure*, 11.
72. North, *Structure*, 19, 44.
73. North, *Structure*, 206.
74. Malthus, *Essay* (1803), 242.
75. Malthus, *Essay* (1803), 330.
76. Malthus, *Essay* (1803), 329.
77. Malthus, *Essay* (1803), 330.
78. Treich, *L'ésprit*, 118.
79. Malthus, *Essay* (1803), 250.
80. Fogel, "Second Thoughts," 31.
81. See Allen, "Great Divergence," 434, fig. 10; Phelps Brown and Hopkins, "Seven Centuries," 311–14; Wrigley and Schofield, *Population History*, 642–44.
82. Malthus, *Essay* (1803), 284.
83. Malthus, *Essay* (1803), 110.
84. Malthus, *Essay* (1803), 89, 282.
85. Malthus, *Essay* (1803), 118 (emphasis in original).
86. Malthus, *Essay* (1803), 241.
87. Malthus, *Essay* (1803), 226, 261.
88. Engels, "Condition of the Working Class," 572–73.
89. Karl Marx, "Critical Marginal Notes," 195 (emphasis in original).
90. Allen, "Great Divergence," 434, fig. 10; Wrigley and Schofield, *Population History*, Appendix 9; Phelps Brown and Hopkins, "Seven Centuries," Appendix B, 311–14. See also Talbot, "The Way We Live Now."
91. See specifically Fogel and others, "Secular Changes," fig. 4, 280. For a general description, see Engels, "Condition of the Working Class."
92. See generally Hobsbawm, *Industry and Empire*, 109–71.
93. Malthus, *Essay* (1803), 282, 285.
94. Malthus, *Essay* (1803), 282. See also Acts 20:35.

95. Malthus, *Essay* (1803), 232–33.
96. Malthus, *Essay* (1803), 234–35.
97. Malthus, *Essay* (1803), 217.
98. Malthus, *Essay* (1803), 120 (emphasis in original).
99. Malthus, *Essay* (1803), 221.
100. Malthus, *Essay* (1803), 122.
101. McEvedy and Jones, *Atlas*, 57; Dupâquier, *Histoire*, 2:67–68; 3:123; Bardet and Dupâquier, *Histoire*, 1:449, 2:290.
102. Livi-Bacci, *Population of Europe*, 9. See also Wrigley and Schofield, *Population History*, 213.
103. Ober, "Wealthy Hellas"; chap. 1 above.
104. Malthus, *Essay* (1803), 252.
105. Malthus, *Essay* (1803), 275–76.
106. Malthus, *Essay* (1803), 245–47.
107. Marx, *Capital*, 1:766, note 6; 1:472–73, note 27. See also Marx, "Theories of Surplus Value," 31:345–52. Marx was referring to the work of the Scottish economists James Anderson and Joseph Townsend. See Steuart, *Inquiry*, first published in 1767.
108. Rubin, *Economic Thought*, 295.
109. Malthus, *Essay* (1803), i, 7.
110. Malthus, *Essay* (1803), 8, 35, 38. See also Süssmilch, *Die göttliche Ordnung*.
111. See Marx, *Capital*, chapter 25, "The General Law of Capitalist Accumulation," 1:762 and following.
112. See Marx, "Theories of Surplus Value," 32:202.
113. See Engels, "Condition of the Working Class," 380, and Engels, "Outlines," 436.
114. See also Marx, *Capital*, 1:1080–81.
115. Pfister, *Bevölkerungsgeschichte*, 43. In the early 1870s, the average age at death of the upper middle class in Liverpool, England, was thirty-five, of the working class, fifteen. Marx, *Capital*, 1:795.
116. Bois, *Crisis*, 400.
117. See for example, "TLC: los campesinos," B4.
118. Babcock, "Concentration of US Agricultural Subsidies."
119. See Goodman, "Bill Clinton's Trade Policies"; "Haiti's President Tries to Halt Crisis"; Qin, "Did Hillary Clinton's State Department"; Robinson, "What the Clintons Did to Haiti"; Weiner, "The Price of Rice Soars"; World Future Fund, "Bill Clinton's Invasion of Haiti."
120. Kennedy, "Riceland Tops Billion Dollar Mark."
121. Engels, "Letter to Friedrich Albert Lange," 136, 137–38.
122. Smith, *Wealth of Nations*, III. iv.10.
123. Floud, "Economics," 241.
124. Compare, for example, Abel, *Geschichte*, 28, to Abel, *Massenarmut*, 26 and following.
125. Malthus, *Essay* (1803), 280.
126. Krugman, "Malthus Was Right!" (emphasis in original).
127. Clark, *Farewell*, 31.
128. Le Roy Ladurie and Goy, *Tithe and Agrarian History*, 191–92. Similarly, Schofield, "Impact," 72, 74; North and Thomas, *Rise*, 132. At least one historian, backed by data, has also rebutted the validity of the Malthusian doctrine for both the medieval and modern periods; see Allen, *Enclosure*, 292–93.

129. Fogel, "Relevance of Malthus," 42.
130. Overton, *Agricultural Revolution*, 63, see also 206.
131. Duby, *Rural Economy*, 120. See also McEvedy and Jones, *Atlas*, 43; Russell; "Late Ancient," 105.
132. McEvedy and Jones, *Atlas*, 43; Overton, *Agricultural Revolution*, 75; Wrigley and Schofield, *Population History*, 642–44.
133. See, for example, Fogel, "Conquest," 33–35.
134. Quoted in Tilly, "Food Entitlement," 135.
135. More, *Utopia*, 130.
136. Sabean, "Social Background," 186; Sabean, *Landbesitz*, 114; see also "Social Background," 5, 6, 37, 60, 129, 158, 159, 185–86, *Landbesitz*, 20, 84, 100, 113, 114; Sabean, "Probleme," 136. See also Konersmann and Troßbach, in Kießling and others, *Grundzüge*, 42–43.
137. Sabean, "Social Background," 161; Sabean, *Landbesitz*, 101 and generally chap. 6 in both texts. See also Endres, "Franken," 136.
138. Rummel, *Bauern*, 317.
139. Campbell and Overton, "A New Perspective," 41.
140. See Ketchmer, "Global Hunger," and Food and Agriculture Organization of the United Nations, "Global Cereal Output" and "Hunger Costs Millions."
141. Cohen, "Pain of Tariffs."
142. See, for example, Becker, "Number of Hungry Rising"; Food and Agriculture Organization of the United Nations, *Food Outlook* and "Global Cereal Output."
143. Cohen, "Pain of Tariffs."
144. Marx, "Theories of Surplus Value," 31:348.
145. Quoted in Hill, *Century of Revolution*, 129.
146. Engels, "Outlines," 436 (translation corrected against the original German).
147. Rintoul, "Farming for the Future."
148. Malthus, *Essay* (1803), 16, 185, 207–08, 325.
149. United States Census Bureau, *Statistical Abstract*, 7.
150. See Overton, *Agricultural Revolution*, 75.
151. Winter, "America Rubs Its Stomach."
152. Egan, "Big Farms."
153. Barrionuevo, "Mountains of Corn."
154. Grimm, *Deutsche Rechtsalterthümer*, 1:345–46; see fuller quote in chap. 7, "Whose forest?"
155. Bertone, "Farm Facts."
156. Streitfeld, "As Prices Rise."
157. Andrews, "Why Isn't Fast Track . . . Faster?"; Becker, "Western Farmers"; Flake, "Bloat Watch"; Becker, "Lawmakers Voice Doom and Gloom On W.T.O. Ruling"; Becker, "W.T.O. Rules Against US"; Egan, "Big Farms"; Barrionuevo, "Mountains of Corn"; Environmental Working Group, *Farm Subsidy Database*. The US also massively subsidizes crop insurance mostly, once again, for the richest agricultural enterprises. Nixon, "Report Says a Crop Subsidy Cap Could Save Billions"; Environmental

Working Group, "Crop
Insurance in the United States."

158. Kautsky, *Agrarian Question*,
214.

159. See, for example, Egan, "Big
Farms."

160. Becker, "US Cutting Food
Aid That Is Aimed at Self-
Sufficiency."

161. Meller, "France Splits With
Europe Over Farm Subsidy
Plan"; *Economist*, "Now
Harvest It." Other articles give
higher figures; Fuller, "For
Farmers in France, No Unity
on Subsidies," lists €53.72
billion for 2004, which is more
than $60 billion.

162. Reuters, "Little Progress."

163. Boulanger, "Les réalités de la
distribution," esp. 8, fig. 4.1,
19; *Economist*, "Europe's Farm
Follies."

164. Bowley, "EU Farm Money."

165. Malthus, *Essay* (1803), 331.

166. Marx and Engels, "Manifesto
of the Communist Party," 482.

•

Sources

ABBREVIATIONS:
  MECW   Karl Marx and Frederick Engels: *Collected Works*
  MEW   Karl Marx and Friedrich Engels: *Werke*

Abel, Wilhelm. *Agricultural Fluctuations in Europe: From the Thirteenth to the Twentieth Centuries*. Translated by Olive Ordish and Joan Thirsk. New York: St. Martin's, 1980.

Abel, Wilhelm. *Geschichte der deutschen Landwirtschaft vom frühen Mittelalter bis zum 19. Jahrhundert*. 3rd ed. Stuttgart: Eugen Ulmer, 1978.

Abel, Wilhelm. *Massenarmut und Hungerkrisen im vorindustriellen Deutschland*. Göttingen: Vandenhoek & Ruprecht, 1972.

Abel, Wilhelm. *Die Wüstungen des ausgehenden Mittelalters*. 3rd rev. ed. Stuttgart: Gustav Fischer, 1976.

Allen, Robert C. *Enclosure and the Yeoman: The Agricultural Development of the South Midlands 1450–1850*. Oxford: Clarendon Press, 1992.

Allen, Robert C. "The Great Divergence in European Wages and Prices from the Middle Ages to the First World War." *Explorations in Economic History* 38 (2001): 411–47.

Allen, Robert C. "Tracking the Agricultural Revolution in England." *Economic History Review* 52.2 (1999): 209–35.

Andrews, Edmund L. "Why Isn't Fast Track . . . Faster?" *New York Times*, 18 August 2002.

Aston, T. H., and C. H. E. Philpin, eds. *The Brenner Debate: Agrarian Class Structure and Economic Development in Pre-Industrial Europe*.

Cambridge: Cambridge University Press, 1987.

Babcock, Bruce. "The Concentration of U.S. Agricultural Subsidies." *Iowa Ag Review online* 7.4 (Fall 2001). http://www.card.iastate.edu/ iowaagreview/fall01/ concentration.aspx.

Bardet, Jean-Pierre, and Jacques Dupâquier, eds. *Histoire des populations de l'Europe*. 2 vols. Paris: Fayard, 1997.

Barrionuevo, Alexei. "Mountains of Corn and a Sea of Farm Subsidies." *New York Times*, 9 November. 2005.

Becker, Elizabeth. "Lawmakers Voice Doom and Gloom on W.T.O. Ruling." *New York Times*, 28 April 2004.

Becker, Elizabeth. "Number of Hungry Rising, U.N. Says." *New York Times*, 8 December 2004.

Becker, Elizabeth. "U.S. Cutting Food Aid That Is Aimed at Self-Sufficiency." *New York Times*, 22 December 2004.

Becker, Elizabeth. "Western Farmers Fear Third-World Challenge to Subsidies." *New York Times*, 9 September 2003.

Bertone, Rachel. "Farm Facts: The United States Farmer." https://www. farmflavor.com/at-home/cooking/farm-facts-the-united-states-farmer/.

Blickle, Peter. *The Revolution of 1525: The German Peasants' War from a New Perspective*. Translated by Thomas A. Brady, Jr., and H. C. Erik Midelfort. Baltimore: Johns Hopkins University Press, 1981.

Bois, Guy. *The Crisis of Feudalism: Economy and Society in Eastern Normandy, c. 1300–1550*. Cambridge: Cambridge University Press, 1984.

Boulanger, Pierre. "Les réalités de la distribution des subventions agricoles en France." https://www.researchgate.net/publication/251290729Lesreali-tesdeladistributiondessubventionsagricolesenFrance.

Bowley, Graham. "EU Farm Money Lands on U.K. Gentry." *New York Times*, 12 April 2005.

Brenner, Robert. "Agrarian Class Structure and Economic Development in Pre-industrial Europe." In *The Brenner Debate*, edited by Aston and Philpin, 10–63.

Brenner, Robert. "The Agrarian Roots of European Capitalism." In *The Brenner Debate*, edited by Aston and Philpin, 213–327.

Campbell, Bruce M. S. "Agricultural Progress in Medieval England: Some Evidence from Eastern Norfolk." *Economic History Review*, n.s., 36.1 (1983): 26–46.

Campbell, Bruce M. S., and Mark Overton. "A New Perspective on Medieval and Early Modern Agriculture: Six Centuries of Norfolk Farming, c. 1250–c.1850." *Past & Present* 141 (November 1993): 38–105.

Cipolla, Carlo M. *Before the Industrial Revolution: European Society and Economy, 1000–1700*. 3rd ed. New York: Norton, 1994.

Clark, Gregory. *A Farewell to Alms: A Brief Economic History of the World*. The Princeton Economic History of the Western World. Vol. 21. Princeton, NJ: Princeton University Press, 2007.

Cohen, Patricia. "Pain of Tariffs Tests Farmers' Faith in Trump: 'How Long Is

Short-Term?'" *New York Times*, 24 May 2019.

Cowell, Alan. "Demographic Time Bomb Threatens Pensions in Europe." *New York Times*, 26 September 2004.

Crouzet, François. "Toward an Export Economy: British Exports During the Industrial Revolution." *Explorations in Economic History* 17.1 (1980): 48–93.

Dees, Robert. *The Power of Peasants: Economics and Politics of Farming in Medieval Germany*. Houston: Commons Press, 2023.

Duby, Georges. *Rural Economy and Country Life in the Medieval West*. Translated by Cynthia Postan. Philadelphia: University of Pennsylvania Press, 1998.

Dupâquier, Jacques, ed. *Histoire de la population française*. Vol. 2: *Des origines de la Renaissance à 1789*. Paris: Presses Universitaires de France, 1988.

The Economist. "Europe's Farm Follies." 8 December 2005. https://www. economist.com/leaders/1997/09/04/europes-farm-follies. (Updated 26 October 2010.)

The Economist. "Now Harvest It." 5 August 2004. https://www.economist.com/ finance-and-economics/2004/08/05/now-harvest-it. (Updated 24 July 2006.)

Edgcumbe, Richard, ed. *The Diary of Frances Lady Shelley, 1787–1817*. London: John Murray, 1912.

Egan, Timothy. "Big Farms Reap Two Harvests With Subsidies a Bumper Crop." *New York Times*, 26 December 2004.

Engels, Frederick. "The Condition of the Working Class in England." In *MECW*, 4:295–583.

Engels, Frederick. "Letter to Friedrich Albert Lange." In *MECW*, 29 March 1865: 42:135–38.

Engels, Frederick. "Outlines of a Critique of Political Economy." In *MECW*, 3:418–43.

Environmental Working Group. "Crop Insurance in the United States." https://farm.ewg.org/cropinsurance.php.

Environmental Working Group. *Farm Subsidy Database*. https://farm.ewg. org/.

Flake, Jeff. "Bloat Watch." *Wall Street Journal*, 2 May 2002.

Floud, Roderick C. "Economics and Population Growth: A Comment." In *Hunger and History*, edited by Rotberg and Rabb, 241–46.

Fogel, Robert W., and others. "Secular Changes in American and British Stature and Nutrition." In *Hunger and History*, edited by Rotberg and Rabb, 247–83.

Fogel, Robert W. "The Relevance of Malthus for the Study of Mortality Today: Long-Run Influences on Health, Mortality, Labor Force Participation, and Population Growth." *NBER Working Paper Series on Historical Factors in Long-Run Growth* 54 (1994).

Fogel, Robert W. "Second Thoughts on the European Escape from Hunger: Famines, Price Elasticities, Entitlements, Chronic Malnutrition, and Mortality Rates." *NBER Working Paper Series on Historical Factors in Long-Run Growth* 1 (1989).

Food and Agriculture Organization of the United Nations (FAO). *Food Outlook* 4 (December 2004). https://www.fao.org/3/j3877e/j3877e00.htm.

Food and Agriculture Organization of the United Nations (FAO). "Global Cereal Output Hits Record High." http://www.fao.org/newsroom/en/news/2004/51844/index.html.

Food and Agriculture Organization of the United Nations (FAO). "Hunger Costs Millions of Lives and Billions of Dollars." https://www.fao.org/asiapacific/news/detail-events/en/c/47177/.

Fuller, Thomas. "For Farmers in France, no Unity on Subsidies." *International Herald Tribune*, 30 June 2005. https://www.nytimes.com/2005/06/30/world/europe/for-farmers-in-france-no-unity-on-subsidies.html.

Godwin, William. *Godwin's "Political Justice": A Reprint of the Essay on "Property," from the Original Edition.* Edited by H. D. Salt. London: Allen & Unwin, 1949.

Goodman, Amy. "Bill Clinton's Trade Policies Destroyed Haitian Rice Farming, Now Haiti Faces Post-Hurricane Famine." Interview with Ninaj Raoul. *Democracy Now!*, 11 October 2016. https://www.democracynow.org/2016/10/11/billclintonstradepoliciesdestroyed.

Grimm, Jacob. *Deutsche Rechtsalterthümer.* 4th ed. Vol. 1. Leipzig: Dieterisch'sche Verlagsbuchhandlung, 1899.

Hansen, Joseph. *Too Many Babies? The Myth of the Population Explosion.* 3rd ed. New York: Pathfinder, 1987.

Henning, Friedrich-Wilhelm. *Handbuch der Wirtschafts- und Sozialgeschichte Deutschlands.* Vol. 1: *Deutsche Wirtschafts- und Sozialgeschichte im Mittelalter und in der frühen Neuzeit.* Paderborn: Ferdinand Schöningh, 1991.

Herlihy, David. *The Black Death and the Transformation of the West.* Cambridge, MA: Harvard University Press, 1997.

Hippel, Wolfgang von. "Bevölkerung und Wirtschaft im Zeitalter des Dreissigjährigen Krieges. Das Beispiel Württemberg." *Zeitschrift für historische Forschung* 5.4 (1978): 413–48.

Hobsbawm, E. J. *Industry and Empire: An Economic History of Britain since 1750.* London: Weidenfeld & Nicholson, 1968.

James, Patricia. *Population Malthus: His Life and Times.* London: Routledge & Kegan Paul, 1979.

Kautsky, Karl. *The Agrarian Question.* 2 vols. London: Zwan, 1988.

Kautsky, Karl. *Der Einfluss der Volksvermehrung auf den Fortschritt der Gesellschaft.* Vienna: Bloch und Hasbach, 1880.

Kennedy, Danny. "Riceland Tops Billion Dollar Mark for 5th Straight Year." *Stuttgart Daily Leader*, 19 November 2012.

Ketchmer, Harry. "Global Hunger Fell for Decades, but It's Rising Again." *World Economic Forum*, 23 July 2020. https://www.weforum.org/agenda/2020/07/global-hunger-rising-food-agriculture-organization-report/.

Kießling, Rolf, Frank Konersmann, and Werner Troßbach. *Grundzüge der*

Agrarwirtschaft. Band 1. *Vom Spätmittelalter bis zum Dreißigjährigen Krieg (1350-1650).* Cologne: Böhlau, 2016.

Krugman, Paul. "Malthus Was Right!" *New York Times,* 25 March 2008.

Le Roy Ladurie, Emmanuel. "A Reply to Robert Brenner." In *The Brenner Debate,* edited by Aston and Philpin, 101–06.

Le Roy Ladurie, Emmanuel, and Joseph Goy. *Tithe and Agrarian History from the Fourteenth to the Nineteenth Centuries: An Essay in Comparative History.* Translated by Susan Burke. Cambridge: Cambridge University Press, 1982.

Livi-Bacci, Massimo. *Population and Nutrition: An Essay on European Demographic History.* Translated by Tania Croft-Murray and Carl Ipsen. Cambridge: Cambridge University Press, 1991.

Livi-Bacci, Massimo. *The Population of Europe: A History.* Oxford: Blackwell, 2000.

Lütge, Friedrich. "Die wirtschaftliche Lage Deutschlands vor Ausbruch des Dreißigjährigen Kriegs." In *Studien zur Sozial- und Wirtschaftsgeschichte, Forschungen zur Sozial und Wirtschaftsgeschichte,* 5:336–95. Stuttgart: Fischer, 1963.

Malthus, Thomas Robert. *An Essay on the Principle of Population.* Selected and introduced by Donald Winch. Cambridge: Cambridge University Press, 1992. (This edition is based on the second, 1803 edition and includes the revisions in the subsequent editions.)

Malthus, Thomas Robert. *An Essay on the Principle of Population, as It Affects the Future Improvement of Society, with Remarks on the Speculations of Mr. Godwin, M. Condorcet, and Other Writers.* London: J. Johnson, 1798. Reprinted. Amherst: Prometheus Books, 1998. (Reprint of the 1798 1st edition.)

Malthus, Thomas Robert. "Principles of Political Economy." In *The Works of Thomas Robert Malthus,* edited by E. A. Wrigley and David Souden, 2nd ed, vol. 5. London: William Pickering, 1986.

Marx, Karl. *Capital: A Critique of Political Economy.* Translated by Ben Fowkes and David Fernbach. Vol. 1. London: Penguin Books, 1976–81.

Marx, Karl. "A Contribution to the Critique of Hegel's Philosophy of Law. Introduction." In *MECW,* 3:175–87.

Marx, Karl. "Critical Marginal Notes on the Article by a Prussian." In *MECW,* 3:189–206.

Marx, Karl. "Theories of Surplus Value," printed as "Economic Manuscript of 1861–63." In *MECW,* 30–33.

Marx, Karl. "Thesen über Feuerbach." Edited by Friedrich Engels. In *MEW,* 3:533–35.

Marx, Karl. "Theses on Feuerbach." In *MECW,* 5:6–8.

Marx, Karl. "Trades' Unions. Their Past, Present and Future." in *MECW,* 20:191–92. Reprinted in Karl Marx and others. *Tribunes of the People and the Trade Unions.* New York: Pathfinder, 2019, 137–40.

Marx, Karl, and Frederick Engels. *Collected Works.* Moscow/New York: Progress Publishers/International Publishers, 1975–2004 (cited as *MECW*).

Marx, Karl, and Frederick Engels. "Manifesto of the Communist Party." In *MECW*, 6:477–519.

McEvedy, Colin, and Richard Jones. *Atlas of World Population History*. New York: Facts on File, 1978.

Meller, Paul. "France Splits With Europe Over Farm Subsidy Plan." *New York Times*, 11 May 2004.

More, Thomas. *Utopia*. Translated by and with an introduction by Paul Turner. London: Penguin, 1965.

Murphy, Brian. *A History of the British Economy, 1086–1970*. London: Longman, 1973.

Mydans, Seth. "Resisting Birth Control, the Philippines Grows Crowded." *New York Times*, 21 March 2003.

Nixon, Ron. "Report Says a Crop Subsidy Cap Could Save Billions." *New York Times*, 11 April 2012.

North, Douglass C. *Structure and Change in Economic History*. New York: Norton, 1981.

North, Douglass C., and Robert Paul Thomas. *The Rise of the Western World: A New Economic History*. Cambridge: Cambridge University Press, 1973.

Ober, Josiah. "Wealthy Hellas." *Transactions of the American Philological Association* 140 (2010): 241–86.

Overton, Mark. *Agricultural Revolution in England: The Transformation of the Agrarian Economy, 1500–1850*. Cambridge: Cambridge University Press, 1996.

Phelps Brown, E. H., and Sheila Hopkins. "Seven Centuries of the Prices of Consumables, Compared with Builders' Wage-Rates." *Economica*, n.s., 23.92 (November 1956): 296–314. Also in *Essays in Economic History*, edited by E. M. Carus-Wilson, 2:179–96. London: Edward Arnold, 1962.

Philp, Mark. *Godwin's Political Justice*. London: Duckworth, 1986.

Pfister, Christian. *Bevölkerungsgeschichte und historische Demographie, 1500–1800*. Munich: Oldenbourg, 1994.

Plato. "Laws." In *Complete Works*, by Plato, edited by John M. Cooper, 1318–1616. Indianapolis: Hackett, 1997.

Qin, Linda. "Did Hillary Clinton's State Department Help Suppress the Minimum Wage in Haiti?" *Politifact*, 21 April 2016. https://www.politifact.com/factchecks/2016/apr/21/lee-camp/did-hillary-clintons-state-department-help-suppres/.

Reuters. "Little Progress Made in Cutting Subsidies." *International Herald Tribune*, 22 June 2005.

Rintoul, Jesse. "Farming for the Future: Why the Netherlands Is the Second Largest Food Exporter in the World." https://dutchreview.com/news/innovation/second-largest-agriculture-exporter/.

Robinson, Nathan. "What the Clintons Did to Haiti." *Current Affairs*, 2 November 2016.

Rösener, Werner. "The Agrarian Economy." In *Germany: A New Social and*

Economic History, 1450–1630, edited by Bob Scribner, 63–83. Vol. 1. London: Arnold, 1996.

Rösener, Werner. *Peasants in the Middle Ages*. Urbana and Chicago: University of Illinois Press, 1992.

Rosenstein, Nathan. *Rome at War: Farms, Families, and Death in the Middle Republic*. Chapel Hill: University of North Carolina Press, 2004.

Rosenthal, Elizabeth. "Nigeria's Population is Soaring in Preview of a Global Problem." *New York Times*, 15 April 2012.

Rotberg, Robert I., and Theodore K. Rabb, eds. *Hunger and History: The Impact of Changing Food Production and Consumption Patterns on Society*. Cambridge: Cambridge University Press, 1983.

Rubin, Isaac Ilyich. *A History of Economic Thought*. London: Pluto Press, 1979, 1989.

Rummel, Walter. *Bauern, Herren und Hexen: Studien zur Sozialgeschichte sponheimischer und kurtrierischer Hexenprozesse 1574–1664*. Göttingen: Vandenhoeck & Ruprecht, 1991.

Russell, J. C. "Late Ancient and Medieval Population." *Transactions of the American Philosophical Society*, n.s., 48.3 (1958): 1–152.

Sabean, David Warren. "German Agrarian Institutions at the Beginning of the Sixteenth Century: Upper Swabia as an Example." In Janos Bak, ed. *The Journal of Peasant Studies* 3.1 (1975): 76–88.

Sabean, David Warren. *Landbesitz und Gesellschaft am Vorabend des Bauernkriegs*. Stuttgart: Fischer, 1972.

Sabean, David Warren. "Probleme der deutschen Agrarverfassung zu Beginn des 16. Jahrhunderts. Oberschwaben als Beispiel." In *Revolte und Revolution*, edited by Blickle, 132–150.

Sabean, David Warren. "The Social Background to the Peasants' War of 1525 in Southern Upper Swabia." PhD diss., University of Wisconsin, 1969.

Scheidel, Walter. "Approaching the Roman Economy: Defining the Roman Economy." In *The Cambridge Companion to the Roman Economy*, edited by Walter Scheidel, 1–21. Cambridge: Cambridge University Press, 2012.

Schofield, Roger. "The Impact of Scarcity and Plenty on Population Change in England, 1541–1871." In *Hunger and History*, edited by Rotberg and Rabb, 67–93.

Smith, Adam. *An Inquiry into the Nature and Causes of the Wealth of Nations*. R. H. Campbell, A. S. Skinner, and W. B. Todd, eds. 2 vols. Oxford: Clarendon Press, 1976.

Sreenivasan, Govind. *The Peasants of Ottobeuren, 1487–1726: A Rural Society in Early Modern Europe*. Cambridge: Cambridge University Press, 2004.

Steuart, James. *Inquiry into the Principles of Political Economy*. Chicago: University of Chicago Press, 1966.

Streitfeld, David. "As Prices Rise, Farmers Spurn Conservation." *New York Times*, 9 April 2008.

Süssmilch, Johann Peter. *Die göttliche Ordnung in den Veränderungen des menschlichen Geschlechts, aus der Geburt, dem Tode und der Fortpflanzung desselben.* Berlin: J. C. Spener, 1741.

Talbot, Margaret. "The Way We Live Now: 6–30–02; The Young and the Restless." *New York Times*, 30 June 2002, Magazine.

Temin, Peter. "The Contribution of Economics." In *Cambridge Companion*, edited by Scheidel, 45–70.

Thompson, E. P. *The Making of the English Working Class.* New York: Vintage Books, 1966.

Tilly, Louise. "Food Entitlement, Famine, and Conflict." In *Hunger and History*, edited by Rotberg and Rabb, 135–51.

"TLC: Los campesinos exigen facilidades." *El Comercio* (Quito, Ecuador), 19 February 2005.

Treich, Léon. *L'ésprit d'Alexandre Dumas.* 2nd ed. Paris: Librairie Gallimard, 1926.

United States Census Bureau. *Statistical Abstract of the United States: 2000.* Washington, D.C.: U.S. Dept. of Commerce, 2000. https://www.census.gov/library/publications/2000/compendia/statab/120ed.html.

Wade, Nicholas. *A Troublesome Inheritance: Genes, Race and Human History.* New York: Kluwer Academic/Plenum Publishers, 2014.

Warde, Paul. *Ecology: Economy and State Formation in Early Modern Germany.* Cambridge: Cambridge University Press, 2006.

Weiner, Tim. "The Price of Rice Soars, and Haiti's Hunger Deepens." *New York Times*, 1 June 2004.

Williams, Gareth. "The Original Anti-Vaxxers: How the Zeal of Edward Jenner Contributed to Today's Culture Wars." *The Economist*, 30 August 2019 (updated 16 September 2020). https://www.economist.com/1843/2019/08/30/the-original-anti-vaxxers.

Wines, Michael. "Malnutrition is Ravaging Niger's Children." *New York Times*, 5 August 2005.

Winter, Greg. "America Rubs Its Stomach, and Says Bring It On." *New York Times*, 7 July 2002.

Wollstonecraft, Mary. *The Love Letters of Mary Wollstonecraft to Gilbert Imlay.* London: Hutchinson, 1908.

World Future Fund. "Bill Clinton's Invasion of Haiti in 1994: Lies, Life and Death." http://www.worldfuturefund.org/Reports/haiti/clintonhaiti.html.

Wrigley, E. A., and R. S. Schofield. *The Population History of England, 1541–1871.* Cambridge, MA: Harvard University Press, 1981.

Index

*A*dvances in agricultural production by farmers powered the great breakthroughs in civilization in Europe: the rise and the overthrow of Rome, the rise of medieval civilization, the overthrow of the feudal ruling classes in England and the Netherlands in the 1300s–1600s, and the ascent of capitalism. Through these revolutions, farmers won greater economic and political freedom, which they put to good use to make the most of nature's bounty.

But winning access to land, liberty, and prosperity required bitter struggles by farmers against the masters of society who, to maximize their own wealth and power, sought to reduce the producers to poverty and servitude.

When farmers were victorious in their fight for greater freedom, whole civilizations advanced; when they were defeated, societies stagnated and collapsed.

Looking at history from the perspective of the farmers and other working people allows us to understand why history took the course it did and better prepares us for battles that lie ahead.

CommonsPress.com ✺ Amazon ✺ Google Play Books ✺ Apple Books
Two-volume set (paperback): US$35 • €33 • £30
Two-volume set (hardback): US$120 • €115 • £100

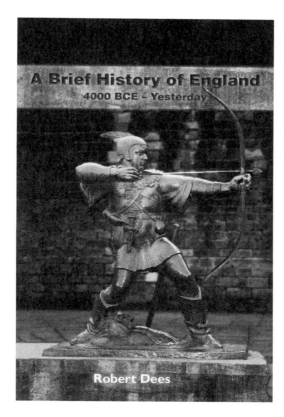

*E*ngland's development from European backwater to world power was the product of its many revolutions. One of the most important of these produced the Forest Charter and its companion, the Magna Carta. Rights won in battle and recognized in these documents were the first steps in the farmers curbing the power of the elites and fighting their way out of serfdom. The creative genius of these now-free farmers produced the soaring increases in agricultural production that powered the rise of a merchant class, towns, manufacturing, trade, and England's rise to world domination.

*W*hen farmers were victorious in their fight for greater freedom, whole civilizations advanced; when they were defeated, as in Germany, societies stagnated and collapsed into more centuries of feudalism and war. Looking at history from the perspective of the farmers and other working people allows us to understand why history took the course it did and better prepares us for battles that lie ahead.